Advanced
Limit Hold'em Strategy
TECHNIQUES FOR BEATING TOUGH GAMES
Barry Tanenbaum

D&B POKER
www.dandbpoker.com

First published in 2007 by D & B Publishing,
PO Box 18, Hassocks, West Sussex BN6 9WR

British Library Cataloguing-in-Publication Data

A catalogue record for this book is available from the British Library.

ISBN: 978 1 904468 363

All sales enquiries should be directed to:
D & B Publishing, PO Box 18, Hassocks, West Sussex BN6 9WR, UK

Tel: +44 (0)1273 711443
e-mail: info@dandbpoker.com,
Website: www.dandbpoker.com

Cover design by Horatio Monteverde.
Printed and bound in the Great Britain by Clays, Bungay, Suffolk.

Contents

Acknowledgements   5

Foreword by Linda Johnson   7

Introduction   11

Part 1 Concepts

1 Predictability   17
2 The Illusion of Action   22
3 Situational Play   25
4 Overcoming Obstacles   44
5 Hand Reading   51
6 Tells   58
7 Raise or Fold   67
8 One Big Bet per Hour   73
9 Balance   84

Part 2 Stages

Section 1 **Pre-flop**

10	Hand Values	90
11	Hand Selection	94
12	Stealing the Blinds	107
13	Blind Play	112

Section 2 **On the Flop**

14	Post-flop Planning	133
15	Reraising on the Flop	147
16	Checking in the Dark	153
17	Common Errors on the Flop	160

Section 3 **On the Turn**

18	Turn Play Overview	166
19	Other Turn Topics	180
20	Raising on the Turn	189
21	Way Ahead or Way Behind	193
22	Playing the Turn from out of Position	198

Section 4 **On the River**

23	River Play Overview	225
24	Raise the Turn or the River	242

Epilogue	246

Acknowledgements

First, I want to thank my wife, the beautiful and talented Betty Tanenbaum. Her patience and support during my whole poker career, and especially while I was writing this book, was beyond wonderful. She also kindly allows me to host a continuous stream of students in our living room. I am extremely lucky to have married an incredible woman.

The people who edited my drafts, Betty (again, who read every page several times) and my friend Matt Kagan, kept me on topic, fixed my errors, and made sure I used proper grammar. It was a huge job, and they performed wonderfully.

Thanks to my publisher, D&B, for taking a chance on my work, and for being so understanding when medical issues kept me from finishing until several months after my promised date.

I also want to offer special thanks to the friends to encouraged my poker career. Nolan Dalla supported me before I had written a word, and recommended me for my first poker writing job. Mark and Tina Napolitano gave me my first chance, allowing me to write for Poker Pages and eventually for Poker School Online as well.

My friends Jan Fisher, Lou Krieger, Linda Johnson (who generously also wrote the foreword to this book), Lee Jones, and Dr. Alan Schoonmaker all offered advice, encouragement and support as I tried to expand my horizons in the poker world. In addition, Terri Evanowski, and all of the members of the Wednesday Poker Discussion Group, patiently listened to my theories and dry run presentations, offering suggestions and invaluable help. Thank you all.

Jan and Linda also invited me to speak at the World Poker Player's Conference for three consecutive years. I really enjoyed creating and delivering the live seminars.

Barry Shulman, Jeff Shulman, and Steve Radulovitch offered me a column with *Card Player* magazine, and later allowed me to write my column for every issue of the magazine. I am honored to be associated with this prestigious publication.

I am a professional poker player because I was able to learn from the works of David Sklansky, Mason Malmuth, Mike Caro, and Bob Ciaffone. I have read many books published since I studied theirs, and I learned from all of them, but the works of these gentlemen formed my game and made me a winning player. To the extent that their ideas are reflected in my book, it is because their theories are the bedrock of my poker knowledge.

Thanks to all of the folks who visit my website, www.barrytanenbaum.com, and a special thanks to the members of my forum who keep the lively and informative dialogue going. After this book is published, we will have a separate topic on the forum for questions and comments about the book and the strategies I recommend here. Also, my great thanks to Shawn Ayre and all of the fine folks at Zelfanet for hosting the website and making it possible.

I also want to thank Terry Borer and Lawrence Mak, who allowed me to collaborate and consult on their new short-handed book, *Limit Hold'em: Winning Short-Handed Strategies.* This excellent work will also have a separate topic on my forum, and Terry and Lawrence have agreed to answer questions and respond to comments there.

Lastly, I want to thank the many people who have written to me, or stopped me in poker rooms, and told me that they have both enjoyed and learned from my writings, lectures, and lessons. Nothing makes me feel more grateful and encouraged than people who take time from their busy days to acknowledge me. It is this more than anything that keeps me writing and teaching.

I hope you feel the same way as they did after you read and implement the ideas in this book. Thank you, readers, for taking the time to consider my ideas.

Foreword

by Linda Johnson

Linda Johnson, nicknamed the First Lady of Poker, has been a leading force in the poker world for much of her life. She played full time from 1980-1993, one of just a handful of women who played the game professionally during those years.

Linda is a co-owner of Card Player magazine, has co-written two poker books and was instrumental in helping to establish many important poker projects including the World Poker Industry Conference, the World Poker Players Conference, and the Tournament Directors Association. Her involvement in promoting poker led to being selected to the Board of Directors for the Poker Players Alliance. She is a partner in Card Player Cruises and has hosted more than 60 poker cruises to destinations around the world.

In 1997 Linda won a gold bracelet in an open event at the World Series of Poker. She teaches poker seminars and hosts tournaments at many cardrooms around the country and has been instrumental in the development of the World Poker Tour. She was the 2005 California State Ladies Poker Champion and the 2006 Orleans Open Woman's Poker Champion.

One of poker's highest honors was bestowed on Linda recently when she was awarded the 2006 Brian Saltus Award, an award given for representing class, dignity, and courage at the poker table.

With the explosion of poker, my life has become quite hectic. As the in-studio announcer for the World Poker Tour and co-owner of Card Player

Cruises, I more often than not am on the road, whether it is filming, hosting a cruise, or lecturing at one of the many poker rooms across the country. During a recent stint at home for the 2006 holiday season, I was delighted to get a phone call from my good friend Barry Tanenbaum asking if I was available to have lunch with him. I jumped at the opportunity.

I knew Barry had been working on a new book, and I was excited to learn more about it. I also was hoping for a sneak peak at what lay in store for the rest of the poker world. What I did not expect was for Barry to ask me to write the foreword for this book... needless to say I was flattered, but also a bit nervous about whether or not I would be able to do justice to the work of this incredible man who I believe is one of the best poker players in the world, and certainly one of the best poker writers.

In Las Vegas, every Wednesday you will find a group of poker players having lunch and talking poker in the back room of Binion's coffee shop. This is where I first met Barry, whom I now consider to be not only a friend, but one of the foremost authorities on limit hold'em. The members of the Wednesday Poker Discussion Group have had the benefit of Barry's keen insight for many years. His contributions to the discussions have made better poker players out of all of us.

In our discussion group, members relate the specifics of difficult hands they played during the week and, as players, give their opinions about how the hand should have been played. You can see that Barry's mind is busy at work. After we have all voiced an opinion, we look to him for the definitive, correct answer. Barry is like E.F. Hutton... when he speaks, everyone listens.

You may not have seen Barry on television because he is primarily a cash game player who has been beating the games for many years. You will often find him in his "office" at The Bellagio, working the late shift and leaving his daytime hours for his many students.

I have had the pleasure of spending countless hours with Barry on our cruises and at the poker tables. It is on the felt that I think a player's true character comes to light, and what impresses me most about Barry is not just his ability to beat the game, it is the manner in which he conducts himself at the table. When you sit in Barry's game, you are his guest, and he is the perfect host, always the gentleman, win or lose.

When Barry first told me many months ago that he was writing a book, my first thought was, "It's about time." My next thought was, "Wow, it's bound to be awesome and I hope my opponents don't read it."

Barry's patient and methodical approach to the game makes him such a wonderful teacher. He has a way of presenting difficult material in such a way that it is easy to understand. Recognizing these wonderful traits, I asked Barry to join me in presenting a mini poker seminar on one of our Card Player Cruises trips to Alaska. Barry impressed me, and all the cruisers who attended the seminar, so I invited him to be a featured speaker at the World Poker Players Conferences in 2003, 2004, and 2005. His presentations are professional, entertaining and fun, and he always receives rave reviews on the attendee surveys. I never miss an opportunity to attend one of Barry's seminars and always learn from them.

I am a World Poker Tour Boot Camp instructor and am often asked if I give private lessons or know anyone I can recommend. I have personally referred more than 40 students to Barry for lessons, and none of them has ever taken me up on my "money back if you aren't satisfied guarantee". His ability to find and address leaks in your game, as well as to break down important poker concepts so you can easily understand and execute them, is why he has earned his reputation as a world-class poker coach. Within this book you will find many important lessons Barry has taught while analyzing not only his play, but that of his students as well. When it comes to teaching poker, Barry is definitely my hero.

Barry's poker credentials extend into printed media as well. As a featured author for *Card Player* magazine, poker players worldwide have reaped the benefits of Barry's experience by reading his thorough, insightful columns.

Every poker player's education should begin with a strong foundation, and every experienced poker player should expand on that education. This book contains many concepts that have never before been explained in print. You will want to read it many times over. When you read the book, you will feel like he is talking directly to you in an easy-to-understand format. I wish this book had been available when I was playing for a living!

Introduction

A few years ago, I was sitting at a $30-$60 table when someone came down from the mezzanine where they keep the higher-limit games. He was in playing the $80-$160 game. He excitedly told his friend playing in my game that the friend had to get on the $80-$160 list, because there was player in it who was playing terribly. The friend asked who it was, and the player pointed to a man who has had more success at the $80-$160 game over the last few years than anyone else in the Bellagio. So they both went to play against him, thinking he did not know how to play.

The fact is that the most successful middle-limit (and higher) players play in a style that is unfamiliar to the average poker player. These experts play and frequently raise with hands that the average player would not consider reasonable, make calls when others might raise, yet still go considerable stretches without playing at all. This, of course, confuses the average player, and makes him believe that the successful player is making all sorts of errors.

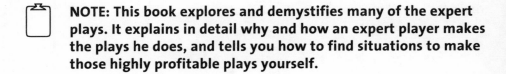 **NOTE: This book explores and demystifies many of the expert plays. It explains in detail why and how an expert player makes the plays he does, and tells you how to find situations to make those highly profitable plays yourself.**

As an example, let's look at pre-flop decisions. The average poker player starts by assessing his hand. He decides if it is worth a raise, call, or fold. If he finds a raising hand, he typically raises if first in or if no one else has raised, and calls if someone else has raised unless he has A-A, K-K, Q-Q, or A-K. With these he reraises. If he has a calling hand, he calls if first in and generally calls if someone has raised in front of him. Only if it is three bets to him does he pause to decide whether he wishes to play. With a folding hand, he folds. Note that this decision is made virtually as soon as he looks at his cards. The main exception comes when he finds himself on the button, and no one has entered the pot. He may now decide to steal, and raise with many hands, sometimes even all of them.

How does an expert player look at the same situation? First, he assesses his position relative to the button. He looks at the blinds, to see how well or poorly they play, and how loose or tight they are. He reviews the other players to see how each is playing, and decides whom he would prefer to play against. He recalls if any have any special characteristics, such as a player who always raises after a bad beat no matter what his cards. He determines what he would like to accomplish when the betting reaches him. He looks to his left to see how the players who are to act after him look at their cards and whether he can tell what actions they are likely to take. He looks right to see what the action is to him.

Then he looks at his cards and decides how the ones he happens to hold fit with his overall concept of the game and how he wishes to play the hand. He mostly still folds, of course, but also calls, raises, or three-bets depending on the action and how the specific players play.

We all start learning hold'em seriously by looking at someone's pre-flop hand chart. The idea that you look at your hand and decide what to do is very ingrained, as it should be. As you can see from the above discussion, the top pro not only considers far more than his cards in making his decisions, he often determines that those factors are more important than the hand he holds.

Of course, talking about cards is far easier than talking about these other factors. But this book emphasizes the non-card related factors that go into making an advanced strategic poker decision. Specifically, we will discuss:

- ♠ Position
- ♠ People
- ♠ Aggression
- ♠ Dead Money
- ♠ Image

This book will improve your limit poker game. If you are a tight player, it will show you how and when to play looser. If you are a loose player, it will show you how and when to play tighter. Overall, this book will make you more money than you make now, or – if you are not yet a winner – it will show you how to stop losing.

If you are beginner, please do not read this book first. Read some basic books and play for a while. I am trying to improve your game, not to give you one.

I assume that you have some idea what ABC poker is like, and are familiar with the general terms and playing styles of the game. I won't waste your time with the basics.

As for me, I am a poker professional, columnist, speaker, coach, and teacher. I have worked with hundreds of students and have heard about thousands of hands played by others. In private lessons, I give advice tailored to the specific needs of each student. For this book, I have taken the most common issues they faced and presented much of the advice I have shared with them.

This book presents concepts and advice for practical implementation. Some of it has appeared in some form in *Card Player* magazine, the cardplayer.com website, and the pokerpages.com web site, but much of the material is new. Some of the hands and discussions also appeared on my website, www.barrytanenbaum.com, and on the forum I host there.

The book is divided into two main parts:

- ♠ Concepts
- ♠ Stages

Part 1, Concepts, deals with your overall approach. It highlights the value of unpredictability, emphasizing that your primary goals are:

1. To be unpredictable.
2. To make your opponents predictable.

The more predictable you can make your opponents, the easier it becomes for you to read hands, make sound decisions, and execute correct situational plays. This book tells you how to accomplish these goals.

Part I also describes the methods top players use to win money in tougher games, working towards winning one big bet per hour or more in middle- and higher-limit games. You may be able to make money in easy games just playing ABC poker, but if you want to make real profits in tougher games, you need to learn to play situations in addition to your cards. You will also learn the importance of balance, which is the key to keeping your opponents guessing about how you play while forcing them into greater predictability.

Part 1, Stages, defines advanced, winning strategies for every street.

Pre-flop

The Pre-flop chapters teach you to assess hand values according to position and the specific situation and determine which opponents to attack and which to avoid. They also tell you when, how often, and from whom you should attempt blind steals, as well as what and how to play when you are in the blinds.

The Flop

The Flop chapters tell you how to plan the play of the hand, and how to execute that plan. They also define the factors that go into your decision of when to raise and reraise. They describe what to do when you are first to act after the flop and discuss the common errors players make and how to avoid them.

The Turn

The Turn chapters tell you what to consider after seeing

the turn card, how that card may affect your plan, and what to do if it does. They review the way you got to the turn, and how to proceed in each case. They provide the factors you need to consider in deciding whether to raise, and how to view your opponents' raises. They define the key principle of "way ahead or way behind", to help you to recognize when it happens, and decide how to play. Finally, this section provides detailed case-by-case analysis of one of the toughest situations in hold'em: playing from out of position on the turn.

The River

The River chapters say why the river is different from every other street, and how you must adapt to those unique conditions. They give you guidelines for when to bet, check, and raise, depending on your position, your opponents, your image, and your hand. Aggression on the river is a key to making extra bets, and here you will learn when to make value bets, and how to respond to them. You will learn when to be aggressive, when to be passive, and the ways to time your raises for the greatest effect.

Overall, your game will become more aggressive, more positional, more geared to your opponent's weaknesses, and, most important, much more profitable.

Part One: Concepts

Chapter One

Predictability

Top poker players use two primary weapons to increase profits:

- ♠ Forcing their opponents into predictability.
- ♠ Being unpredictable themselves.

Winning poker players simply make more good decisions than losing ones. And making decisions is easiest when your opponents are predictable.

Let me give you a couple of examples from televised poker. I am using them so everyone has a common reference. In the first case, a well-known star raises pre-flop, and an unknown player comes over the top. The poker star folds, but is that all he does? No, he also delivers a lecture about how risky the reraise was and how the star next time would have a better hand and take all of the unknown player's chips. At another table, another star player raises pre-flop, and an unknown player comes over the top. At this table the star now stares at the unknown for at least a full minute, looking at him with an unwavering glare. Finally he folds.

The lecture and the stare down both have the same objective: to make the unknown player predictable. Each star, in his own way, was trying to make the unknown think, "Wow, that guy is tough. If I bluff him, he will see right through me and take all my chips. I had better stay away from him unless I have a really good hand."

Since the pro plans to raise often, and does not want the unknown reraising with weak hands, he has accomplished his purpose. First, the unknown will avoid confrontations with him without a very good hand, which will make it easier for the star to steal blinds, antes, and whole pots. Second, when the unknown does reraise, the star can get away from his hand more easily, knowing that unknown player has a quality hand. Of course, this next laydown will be accompanied by another lecture/stare-down, just to reinforce the point.

Well, that's interesting but what does it have to do with us? Simply put,

 TIP: The primary strategic objective of top poker players is to make their opponents predictable while remaining unpredictable themselves.

Why is predictability important? The key to advanced poker is reading hands. You read them based on your opponents' betting patterns (and physical tells, which I am not dealing with right here). If you have a predictable opponent, his actions let you put him on a narrow range of hands, which helps you to make better decisions. Better decisions equal a fatter wallet.

Once in a while, your opponents will be predictably wild (maniacs), but even they are fairly easy to play; you may not know what they have, but you do know what they will do. You can get them to help you to build pots when you want them large, or you can try to play passively to keep them small. You can check and call or check-raise, knowing they will bet.

But most opponents are not wild; they try to play well. To them, playing well means following a certain series of rules known only to them. If you can crack their code, you have a significant advantage. To do this, you need to make opponents predictable.

To keep your sharper opponents from cracking your code, you must at least appear to be unpredictable. One of the greatest compliments a winning player can receive is to hear a sophisticated player say, "I never know what to put you on."

As you can see by the no-limit tournament discussion, one way to make opponents predictable is to have them fear you. Some players act obnoxious to get that fear factor operating, but that kind of behavior is –EV in the long run; it drives weak opponents away from them and possibly from the game in general.

You are better off sowing both fear and confusion by your betting and table image in general. I call this concept "FUD".

FUD

I want to take a moment and explain FUD. It's a term that was developed by IBM in the 1960s when several competitors were developing rival computers. In general, every rival computer was better than an IBM because it had to be better. None of them tried to compete against IBM with an inferior machine.

IBM's marketing strategy to counter these superior products was called "FUD", which stood for *Fear, Uncertainty, and Doubt*. The idea was to convince the market and particularly corporate officers that, if you buy a non-IBM machine, who knows what might happen? Maybe it won't be good. Maybe it will get bad service. If you go with IBM, you know you are getting a great machine, great service, great parts, and great support. If you went with anybody else, you were venturing into the unknown. We used to have a slogan: "Nobody ever got fired for buying an IBM computer." FUD worked wonders.

 TIP: FUD is a poker player's best friend.

To be a top player, you must spread fear, uncertainty, and doubt among your opponents. You want them to be afraid of you. You want them to misunderstand you. You want them to be confused about exactly where you are. Opponents who are afraid, confused, and disoriented tend to become predictable. They can't make a move against you because they don't know where you are, so they tend to become passive, mostly folding, checking, and calling. They bet and raise only when they have real hands, and they seldom bluff. In short, they become more predictable.

If you are a rock, you inspire fear, but not uncertainty and doubt. When you raise, opponents think things like, "Oh. I better avoid him." "I'm not going to play my Q-10 offsuit against this guy." "I will fold my K-J suited in the blind." You generate the fear factor, but you don't create any uncertainty or doubt because they feel comfortable that they know what you are playing.

If you are a loose-aggressive player, or even a loose player, you inspire uncertainty and doubt. You play a lot of hands, so people don't know exactly what you have, but you don't create fear. People don't get nervous because you play, or even raise, because it's just part of the overall flow of the game. Opponents realize you are going to play or raise with A-K and A-5 and K-Q and J-9 suited, so nobody fears these raises or plays. Nobody thinks, "Oh, my God, he's in the hand! I don't want to play." Opponents feel comfortable reraising you and betting into you with a wide range of hands. This makes them unpredictable, making it difficult for you to read their hands.

You want to balance fear and uncertainty and doubt. Play tightly enough to inspire fear, but be varied enough to create substantial uncertainty and doubt in your opponents' minds. Doing this will have two effects:

- ♠ They will become more predictable, because afraid, uncertain opponents tend to be more predictable.
- ♠ They will often pay off your big hands, which you will hold most of the time you play.

You want to create enough action so that there is at least some uncertainty and doubt in your opponents' minds about whether you really have a hand this time. At the same time, you almost always want to have a real hand. Don't act like an idiot just to create uncertainty.

You can create this uncertainly by:

- ♠ Playing looser in late position.
- ♠ Raising and three-betting more often.
- ♠ Playing some draws aggressively.
- ♠ Value betting the river aggressively.

The FUD concept requires striking a balance between fear, uncertainty, and doubt. Keep your opponents off-balance and uncertain about where they can put you. Make them understand that you are likely to turn over a good hand, but you might not, so they sometimes have to pay you off.

If you don't make those plays, if you don't make those three-bets, if you don't show an occasional weaker hand or a called bluff, you become a player who can't make much money in tougher games. You may find yourself saying, "I am a disciplined player. I should be beating these guys for more than I am," and wondering why you aren't.

Inverse FUD

You can also use the FUD concept to assess your own game. For every player, decide how much FUD you are feeling about him. On rare occasions, you will find a table that is FUD-free, but generally, you will find some degree of fear, uncertainty, and doubt in your own mind related to one or more of your opponents.

A certain amount of FUD is reasonable, of course, as you are unlikely to feel in control of everyone. However, if you realize that you feel FUD towards many opponents, it is time to find another game.

Continuously monitoring your personal FUD factor allows you to determine when to stay at a table and when to leave far better than any other measure.

Conclusion

1. Predictability is a critical factor in winning hold'em.
2. Try to make your opponents predictable.
3. Make your play unpredictable.
4. Creating FUD can accomplish 2 and 3.

Chapter Two

The Illusion of Action

The *"Illusion of Action"* means making enough plays that look like action (while generally still having positive expectation) that you get real action from opponents when you have the best of it. *Illusion of Action* is one way to create FUD, and it is the primary method used in tough limit games by top players.

In loose or weak games, or against unaware opponents, you may play tight and get plenty of action. If so, you don't need any help because you are getting what you want. You are playing premium hands and getting paid off. There are many such games. Interestingly, a student told me, "I sat there for an hour, then played a hand, and the guy on my left said, 'You haven't played a hand in an hour! I call.' " In a game like that you don't have to expand your game to make a significant profit.

As you move up in stakes or just find yourself in games with observant opponents, sitting for an hour and then playing a hand does not get you much action. You need to do something to manufacture profits. Specifically, you need to exploit your tight image by making an occasional play with weaker cards, expecting that opponents will roll over and give you the pot. When they do, you make money. When they don't, and you happen to show them a substandard hand, you have created FUD. By becoming unpredictable in their eyes, you will now reap the benefits by getting paid on your powerful hands, which is mostly what you play.

You don't want to stop playing a primarily tight, aggressive style. The question is, can you expand your game so that you are still primarily in +EV[1] situations, but get action? Tight players get too much respect.

 NOTE: There is no point in being a tight player if you don't use your tight image to win pots that you don't deserve.

The problem with tight players is that they rarely win any pots they don't deserve because they are in with only premium hands, and they deserve the pots they win. They are playing A-A and K-K and A-K, but everybody plays A-A and K-K and A-K. They are not generating any additional revenue, and they are not inducing action on their big hands.

If you are a tight player, learning to use the *Illusion of Action* is the most important weapon you can add to your arsenal. You want the image that you are providing action to the extent that people will not think you are a rock. On the other hand, you don't want to create action just for the purpose of creating action because you don't want to put yourself in –EV situations. How do you do this?

Sometimes you can do it by playing naturally, but sometimes you need to take some extra steps. These include:

- ♠ Use position more effectively.
- ♠ Exploit the weaknesses of your opponents.
- ♠ Become more aggressive.
- ♠ Actively create dead money.
- ♠ Use your image to win extra money.

Here is one example:

Using this method, I held Q♦-9♦ in the cutoff. A tight, losing, frustrated

---

[1] "EV" stands for expected value, which is a measure of profitability over the long run. Situations that are profitable over many iterations are considered "+EV", while those that are long-term losers are "–EV". Most casino games have a built-in house edge, and are therefore –EV for the player. In poker, your goal is to determine which situations are +EV, and play only in those circumstances.

player open-raised on my right. He seemed to be a good candidate for a play because he seemed impatient to play a hand, but sufficiently defeated that he would not make any fancy plays.

I three-bet to gain position (buy the button), make the blinds fold (dead money), and win the battle of aggression. I did not think I had the best hand, but in this situation, I felt I could wrestle the pot away from this opponent often enough to show a good profit. And, if not, I would sow seeds of doubt if I happened to show down a hand like Q-9 that I had three-bet.

On the flop of J♣-6♦-3♥ he checked and I bet. He called, which bothered me a bit, as I was hoping to win it right there. The turn was the 9♥, so at least I now had something. Again check, bet, call. He should have given up on A-K and A-Q by then, so I had to worry about a hand like K-J or 10-10 or even Q-Q. He could also have 7-7 and been hoping I had A-K.

The river was the 2♣, and he checked again. I like to bet the river, but I thought there were more hands that would beat me than hands I could beat, and I did not want to get check-raised. I checked. He showed down K-Q, so my pair of nines won.

What did I accomplish?

♠ I won the pot.

♠ I showed my opponents that I had three-bet with Q-9. That should get me some FUD extra play when I three-bet with premium hands later in the session.

♠ I looked like a foolish player because the table saw my weak three-bet. Also, it looked like I got lucky because I hit my kicker, whereas, in reality, I was going to win that pot almost all the time whether I hit my nine or not. If I had missed on the turn and river, I was going to bet, and he would have folded K-Q. In fact, he would not have called the turn if the nine did not give him a gutshot.

Of course, I could not use that play again for quite a while with those players. But my play left the opponents confused and afraid, which increased both my subsequent action and the errors they made.

The next chapter details how to accomplish the *Illusion of Action* by playing situationally.

Chapter Three

Situational Play

The vast majority of winning players wait for hands that have positive expectation, and then put in many bets. This is the essence of the selective-aggressive philosophy that has been proven over the years to be a winning one.

I agree with it, and I have profited significantly doing exactly that against players who lose patience, take the worst of it, gamble to excess, or simply cannot separate +EV hands from minus ones.

If you play a selective-aggressive style and have patience, you can beat most games because they contain enough bad players. Waiting to have the best of it against poor players who can't get away from hands is the bedrock method of making money at limit hold'em.

Bluffing

Let's go off on a tangent for a moment and talk about bluffing. Bluffing is an essential part of the game. If you never bluff you become predictable, and your smarter opponents will simply stop paying you off. However, if you play opponents who will pay you off whether you bluff or not, you should not bluff.

Eventually, most opponents will realize that you never bluff, and you will find it hard to get action on your winning hands. You can stop there and just live with the decreased profit, partially because bluffing costs you money when you try and fail. If you stop bluffing, you sacrifice the significant profit that comes from winning pots when your bluff is successful, AND you give up the extra calls you would get once your opponents realize that your bet might be a bluff.

If you realize this, you will bluff at least occasionally, not to show that you can bluff, but because in the long run a proper bluffing strategy (or even a less proper but occasional bluffing strategy) will be +EV.

When you bluff, your cards at that moment are not +EV, *but you play them in a way that creates added value.* You hope to win the pot by betting, but even if you don't win now, you gain long-term expectation because your value bets in future hands have a greater chance of getting paid off.

That is how bluffing works. Occasionally you bet with the worst hand in an attempt to win the pot, and sometimes you win it. If you don't, you lose extra money on that hand, but probably make it back in the long run because of the FUD you have planted in your opponents' minds.

Situational play

What would happen if you extended that philosophy into other situations? In fact, what about looking for situations in which your actual hand is not as important as the fact that you may be able to win the pot by brute force, and if not, you may get action later?

You would now be making plays with hands that are not +EV (in fact, your specific hand may not even be relevant), but the situation is +EV. These situations would require your putting in many more bets than a single bluff, and, if you fail, you would lose considerable money. You would need to be able to tolerate considerable swings. If you can't even tolerate losing a single bet when you bluff unsuccessfully, then this strategy is not for you. In fact, as we will discuss in Chapter 4 – Overcoming the Obstacles to Success, learning to tolerate swings and losses is a major step towards increasing profits.

Like bluffing, if these plays work often enough to show a profit or even a small loss, but increase your action on your better hands, then you gain from this approach.

There is no need to do this if your opponents are paying you off. And like bluffing, you need to do it sparingly, with the right opponent, and when you have the right image.

Time for an example.

Example

I was at the Rio during the World Series of Poker killing a few hours. I jumped into a $20-$40 game that was just forming. After 10 minutes, it was clear the game was playing very tightly, as many games do when they start. We were seven-handed, and I held K♦-3♦ on the button. The early players folded, and a tight gentleman limped from the cutoff. I didn't think anyone open-limped from the cutoff anymore, but he did. Certainly that meant he did not have a premium hand or even anything close, so I raised. My objective was to create a situation where he would have to hit the flop or give me the pot containing 6½ small bets, assuming the blinds folded.

This time the big blind did not fold, and the cutoff called. I flopped a king and bet out three times, the blind calling all the way and the cutoff folding on the flop. I won the showdown over the big blind's pocket eights. If the big blind had a lesser hand, I would have won on the flop whether I hit my hand or not, providing he did not hit his.

After the hand, the cutoff turned to me and told me he had A♣-6♣. His point was that I was stupid raising with K-3 when he was smart enough to limp in with A-6. I'm sure many players feel that way, but I was happy with my actions and the prospect of later profits if I should happen to raise pre-flop with a real hand. I was also happy with the fact that he thought I was a poor player, as that would lead him to make additional errors during the session.

I was reminded of something that I heard once in a bridge tournament, "The losers all go home complaining about the terrible play of the winners."

Key factors in situational play

To make a situational play, you need the following elements:

1. **Position**. This is critical. You will have a very hard time being successful playing out of position without a real hand.
2. **The right opponent**. You must select an opponent who:
   a. Has a high probability of not holding a premium hand,
   b. Will not try fancy plays, so you can safely fold if he bets and you miss the flop, and
   c. Will call you down only if he makes something.
3. **Aggression.** You must take the lead and keep it as long as there is a chance your hand is good, or the opponent will fold.
4. **Dead money.** You prefer to have just a single opponent. Not only because one is much easier to beat, but if there is extra money in the pot left there by current non-combatants, that money can be shared between you and the opponent in proportion to how often you each win the hand. This turns some situations in which you will win less than half the time into +EV for both of you.
5. **Image.** You can't play this way if people expect it. So this is not a good method if you are a maniac and loose player. It works best when used sparingly, just enough to keep people from trusting you entirely.

1. Position

We all understand the general concept of position. Late position is good and you can play more hands. Early position is bad, and you should play fewer hands. But you need to go well beyond that to make extra money.

You have your own playing style, and you need to decide what your overall approach to the game is. If you are a tight player who is having trouble winning enough, then you need to loosen your game by playing more hands in position, and being more aggressive. If you are a loose player who is losing, or winning a small amount, because you are playing too often with the worst of it, then you need to tighten up in early position and in the blinds, so you are not faced with so many difficult out-of-position decisions.

I want to emphasize again that if you are doing well, making good money, and in particular getting your better hands paid off, then please keep doing what you are doing and look at this section as an interesting theoretical discussion.

We will look at position play from the following perspectives:

- ♠ Absolute versus relative
- ♠ Pre-flop
- ♠ Post-flop

Absolute versus relative

Because position is so important, you need to be aware of your position throughout the hand. Of course, at the start of the hand, you know your position relative to the button, and that does not change. We call that your *absolute position*.

But during the hand, you may find yourself facing a bet with several players to act behind you. In this case, despite what your absolute position may be, you would be effectively under the gun for that betting round. Your position relative to the bettor becomes much more important than your position relative to the button, which we call your *relative position*.

Example

You are on the button in a $20-$40 game. Two middle position players limp, and the cutoff raises. You are thinking of calling with K♥-Q♣. You believe the raiser may be raising with a wide variety of hands trying to buy the button and gain position on the two limpers.

Let's think ahead. Assume you call, and the big blind calls, as do the two limpers. Now there are 10½ bets in the pot. The flop comes A♠-10♣-5♦, giving you a gutshot for the nuts. Everyone checks to the cutoff, who bets. You are now getting 11.5-to-1 on a 10.75-to-1 draw. This sounds like a fine call, especially considering implied odds. And it would be if your call closed the betting, but there are three players yet to act, and one or more of them may choose to check-raise. If, after you call, there is a raise and a call to you, you would again be getting the right price in installments and have to call, but overall you would have paid two bets to win 14, thus taking way the worst of it. And of course it would be worse with a raise and a reraise after your call.

If you call the flop with this hand, you are gambling that there will be no raises, and that's not good poker. You should fold, though few players would. But the root cause of the problem was your pre-flop call. Even though you had the button, you could anticipate that everyone would likely check to the raiser and that the raiser would bet, thus giving you the worst possible relative position on that betting round.

Understanding the concept of relative position and anticipating what your position may be on each betting round can improve your decision-making on earlier rounds.

How should you have played the hand? You could recognize that before the flop you were in a "raise or fold" situation[2]. As our example showed, even if you received a reasonably favorable flop, you faced a very difficult decision. You can avoid that by either folding, thus avoiding the problem, or three-betting. In addition to possibly creating dead money, to be discussed later in this chapter, you would have significantly increased your likely relative position. On the same flop, if everyone checks to you, you can take the free card for the nuts with no risk of raises behind you.

Certainly, it does not have to play out that way, and if the other players are aggressive bettors who will not almost always check to the raiser, you should not make the play. But raising or folding would be an improvement over calling and accepting poor relative post-flop position.

This concept comes up frequently. For example, you are in the big blind contemplating calling a raise in a multiway pot. You should be more

---

[2] This will be defined and detailed in Chapter 7.

inclined to call that raise if it came from under the gun (taking into account the strength that raise may be showing) than if the raise came from the button. In the first case, the UTG player will likely bet the flop, giving you excellent relative position. Also, your call closes the betting on this round. If the raise comes from the button, your call may still be subject to a reraise behind you. Plus, after the flop, your relative position on the flop will be poor if everyone checks and the button bets.

Pre-flop

Before the flop, if you are in early position relative to the blinds, you have no idea how the hand will play out. Will it be multiway? Will it be heads-up? Will there be several raises or none at all? Will the weaker players be in or will the better players? You have absolutely no idea. Yes, you can assert that events in the past have predictive value, and in poker sometimes they do. And if you believe they are totally reliable, you can act as if they have already happened. For example, a maniac may be in your game who will raise every time. Or your game may be so loose that nearly everyone has seen every flop for the past hour, no matter whether there was a raise or not. In these cases, you should certainly use your judgment and play hands that fit the criteria of that specific game. Usually, though, your game will not have this predictability. The only thing you can be certain of is that it is your turn and anything may happen.

You should therefore play squeaky tight in early position. You cannot play your relative position because you don't have any. You cannot play the players because you do not know which players you may be facing. So you have to play your cards. Restrict yourself to A-A through 10-10, A-K and A-Q. Open-raise with them. Does this make you exploitable when small cards hit? No, because almost half the time you will have an overpair, so opponent cannot simply assume you have overcards and make a play.

If you follow these guidelines, you will raise 30 times with pairs (six ways to make A-A, K-K, Q-Q, J-J, 10-10) for every 32 times with big cards (16 for A-K and 16 for A-Q)[3]. This sounds balanced to me.

---

[3] The math works as follows. For each pair, say aces, there are four in the deck, and six ways they can be combined: Spades-hearts, spades-diamonds, spades-clubs, hearts-diamonds, hearts-clubs, and diamonds-clubs. For each overcard combination, say ace-king,

As you get closer to the button, you can play more hands. Which ones will depend on your game, and your assessment of the players to act after you and in the blinds. If you are looking at implementing the *Illusion of Action* discussed in the previous chapter, use the last three positions in a full ring game to expand your normal hand selection and your aggression level.

Example

You are in the cutoff with J♥-10♥. Two average players limp in front of you. Normally, this is an easy call, with good position and a volume hand. But raising cannot be a terrible play, and certainly will label you as an action player if you happen to show your hand. (Even if you don't show it, raising in spots like this will increase your raising frequency overall, and your more observant opponents will note your "looseness".) The raise may buy you the button, knock out the blinds, or make the pot larger for your volume hand, and possibly set you up for a steal if you need to represent an ace or a king later in the hand. If it happens to attract callers, that is OK, too, as you hold a hand that tends to play well in a multiway pot.

Note that I said the last *three* positions, not the last two. In addition to making plays on the button or the cutoff, the spot in front of the cutoff, which I call the *power position* (I have heard it called the "trigger" or "hijack" position, more on this in Chapter 12) offers excellent opportunities to expand your game while retaining credibility.

While you still need to be careful, here is where you can draw the line between playing a reasonably snug game and a fairly loose one if you need to. If the blinds are tight, and the remaining players rarely three-bet, you can expand your game in the power position. By that I mean open-raising with hands like any two Broadway cards, suited aces to A-7, A-9 offsuit, K-9 suited, and pairs down to 6-6. This is not the play you make every time you see these hands, as folding is generally a reasonable option, but raising here pressures the blinds and players behind you to

there are four of each type, and sixteen ways they can be combined: Each ace with each of the four kings. Thus, A-A can be dealt six ways compared to sixteen ways for A-K.

have very good hands to play with you.

With a single limper to you, you can still raise with these hands to create the *Illusion of Action*, as long as the limper is neither tight nor tricky. By tight I mean someone who limps with hands like A-Q and A-J instead of hands like 8-8 and Q-Js. By raising, you force a straightforward opponent to make a hand or fold. Since you are also raising with your premium hands, you are creating FUD when you do occasionally show down a hand that others in your game may consider somewhat over the top.

Example

For example, an opponent limps in middle position with Q♠-J♠. You now raise with J♥- 10♥, and everyone else folds. In theory you are dominated, but in practice, your opponent has to make a hand to win. If the flop is A♣-6♣-5♦ or 7♠-7♥-4♣, he will almost always check and fold. After all, how can he call you down with queen-high? He doesn't know that he has you dominated; in fact, he might reasonably surmise that you dominate him. Sometimes you will lose, of course, but you will profit in the long run from a combination of:

- ♠ The number of times you simply win on the flop.
- ♠ The times you get lucky (the flop is J♦-10♦-4♣ and you get paid off).
- ♠ The action you will get later on your premium hands because you make an occasional play like this.

You can also reraise certain middle position raisers from the last three positions with less than premium hands if you need to show some action. If you believe your opponent is someone who will raise with many hands in late position, you can reraise and create the same effect. I do not like to give up position to a loose raiser, and reraising provides far more benefits than calling does.

Does this mean you can reraise with hands like 7-2 suited and 9-3 offsuit, since you are trying to win without a showdown? I don't recommend it. It's nice to have some reasonable way to win (Q-8 suited plays decently against 6-6, 7-2 does not) and you will have to win occasional showdowns regardless of your plans and desires. If you pick up 8-3, give it up and wait for a better hand. In general, reserve *Illusion of Action* pre-flop reraises to hands you would have liked to play pre-flop if not for the raise in front of you. Then, if the right opponent is raising, and the right players are behind you and in the blinds, make the play. Having reasonable criteria, even for your unusually aggressive image plays, will keep you from making these plays too often.

Post-flop

When you see the flop, you know 71.4% of your final hand. This is certainly enough for you to flesh out your plan for how to play your hand. Even before anyone bets, think about where you are and how you want to play. Ask yourself the standard questions:

- ♠ Do I have a made hand, a draw, or nothing?
- ♠ Based on the betting, what are my opponents likely to have?
- ♠ Do I want to build a pot or keep it small?
- ♠ Do I want to keep opponents in or eliminate them?

There are also some less standard questions you should ask:

- ♠ What sorts of hands can I represent?
- ♠ How likely is a bluff?
- ♠ Do I have or can I gain the lead, so opponents have to react to my plays?
- ♠ Should my overall approach be active or passive?

Don't forget that if you are out of position after the flop, you have information that you did not have about your opponents' hands before the flop. Pre-flop, you knew only that they had two cards. Now you know how they acted on those cards, and you must account for that as you play your hand.

I will discuss this post-flop thinking further in Part II, when I go through the play street by street.

2. The Right Opponent

You must understand your opponents, not only so you can read their hands, but also to understand their motivations. For example, someone who has lots of money but is in your game just to have fun is more likely to call on the end than one who is tight on cash and trying to make frugal decisions. You can learn a lot about your opponents by talking to them.

Dr. Alan Schoonmaker, in his book *Psychology of Poker*, did an excellent job of defining the four primary types of opponents you will meet: loose-passive, loose-aggressive, tight-passive, and tight-aggressive.[4] For our purposes, you need to go beyond those descriptions, and the more insight you can gather, the better. Not that this identification method is a bad place to start – it's not. You must be able to identify the basic inclinations of each player. You can't stop there, though.

You need to understand how players react on each street. For example, some loose-passive players will call the flop with nothing at all, hoping they can still make a hand. Some will fold if they miss. If you are thinking of continuing your aggression on the turn, it helps to know which one you are facing.

Some tight-aggressive players will automatically raise on the flop if they raised pre-flop and you bet into them. Some raise only with their best hands. Conversely, some raise with overcards and wait for the turn to raise with their better holdings. You just can't say, "He's a tight-aggressive player," and think you have summed up his style.

Some tight-passive players will almost never lay down a hand. They waited a long time, and they want to see what they are losing to. You want to value bet them if possible. Others pride themselves on hand reading and get great pleasure from not paying you off. You can bluff these players if you play in such a way that they will "get a read" on what you have when you actually have something else. I call this play the "read-bluff".

---

[4] Dr. Schoonmaker greatly expands on this concept and many more in his recent book, *Your Worst Poker Enemy*.

Some players lead with flush draws, some never do. Some check-raise the flop only with two pair, some only with top pair, some with top or middle pair, some with draws.

Some players bet the river with any decent hand. Some bet only with two pair or better, and check when a flush card comes unless they made the flush themselves. This may sound silly to you if you don't play like this, but you can't assume others share your theory of the game. You need to figure out *their* theory of the game and adapt to it.

Unfortunately, there is no shortcut to deciding who plays how. You watch and learn. More exactly, you watch and form tentative conclusions, and then look for confirmation or refutation, which allows you form new and improved hypotheses.

Most important, if you wish to implement *Illusion of Action* plays, you are looking for the following types:

- ♠ Tight players who limp late.
- ♠ Action players who raise liberally pre-flop in late position.
- ♠ Hyper-aggressive players who raise liberally in middle position.
- ♠ Bad players who limp with too many hands.
- ♠ Predictable players who let you know when you are behind.
- ♠ Players who will fold on the flop or turn with overcards if they have no hand.

All of these players are vulnerable to in-position aggression, as they will generally give up their hands easily if they miss, or let you know if you are behind. In the case of the hyper-aggressive player, he is so likely to be behind your above-average holdings that you will have the best hand and the best position much of the time.

3. Aggression

Most of the books correctly agree that aggression is important, but let's examine what aggression is.

To some players, aggression means all-action-all-the-time. Just bet and raise when it is your turn and put maximum pressure on everyone.

Short-handed, this has some merit, but in a full game, it's deadly. You will find yourself against just the one or two players who hold real hands time after time, and they will call you down.

To others, aggression means waiting for a really good hand or the near nuts and raising. These players also feel like they are aggressive, though what they really are is predictable and easy to read. Again, if you are raising with your top hands only and still getting plenty of action, your opponents are not reacting properly and you should simply keep doing what you are doing.

Meaningful aggression falls between these two extremes. You must be betting and raising with some draws and questionable hands as well as with the nuts, but you also have to slow down when you may be beat, or when betting and raising will not gain you anything. As we have seen already, you should make those aggressive plays in position and against the right players.

Example

You have pocket kings in the cutoff. A middle position player raises and you three-bet. Only he calls. The flop comes A-A-3. He checks, and you bet. He calls. The turn is a 6. He checks again. Should you bet?

I saw this situation played out twice in two weeks, and both times the players with pocket kings bet. I think this is a case of misplaced aggression. This clearly meets the definition of a way-ahead-or-way-behind situation. You have no idea if you are ahead or not. If behind, you have almost no outs, and, if ahead, your opponent has almost no outs.

I understand that if you check and your opponent would have folded to a bet, your check is a significant error. But if you bet and get check-raised, you will have made a symmetrical error. And the chances of getting check-raised are very real. In both hands I witnessed, the turn bet was check-raised. One player correctly folded his kings, but his bet opened him up for a bluff and eliminated his chances to hit a king on the river. The other player called and did hit his king, getting undeservedly lucky. Both players could have seen the river for free, and seen their opponent's hand for the same bet they used on the turn.

Aggression does not simply mean betting when it's your turn. Poker is closer to chess: you need to figure out what moves to make in advance of making them. Have a good reason for your actions, and make sure they fit your overall plan for the hand.

If you are using *Illusion of Action* plays, err on the aggressive side. If you think it's close between a bet and a check, bet. If you think it's close between a call and a raise, raise. No one ever folded to a check or a call. This does not mean you can abandon poker logic and just pick the most aggressive play, but if you want to inspire FUD, a bit of extra aggression goes a long way.

4. Dead Money

"Dead money" is the money left in the pot by players who are no longer in contention for the pot. It represents equity that is shared by the players remaining in the hand in addition to the money they themselves have contributed. Of course, if everyone folds, then the entire pot consists of dead money plus the contribution of the winner.

Develop a love of dead money. It is worth extending yourself a bit to create it.

Example

I raised in early position in a Las Vegas $30-$60 game with A-Q and was called by a fairly tight player. I felt that the fact that he did not three-bet was significant. The somewhat loose button player reraised and the blinds folded. This was great, as already we had made $50 of dead money to be shared among the three of us. However, I was looking for more. The question was, if I raised again, would the tight player fold and abandon the $60 he had already bet? Most players would chase that money to the death, but I thought that he would release about half the time. My hand was on the minimum side for my early position raise, but you already know that I look well beyond my hand in assessing situations. Also, there was the danger of being raised again because four bets is not a cap in Las Vegas.

I love dead money, though, so I did put in the fourth bet, and the tight player indeed folded. The loose button called.

Let's look at what has happened. The pot contained 11.66 bets, of which the button and I put in four each, with 3.66 dead. If I put in five more small bets (equal to calling every street) and win only 42% of the time, I would still show a tiny profit. I could afford to be a 58-42 underdog and still make a profit thanks to the dead money in the pot. I expected to win even more often than that.

Dead money is critical to *Illusion of Action* players, and it is one of the reasons for the occasional extreme pre-flop and sometimes post-flop raising. If someone raises, and you reraise, that is sometimes called an "isolation play", in that you are trying to get heads-up. From my perspective, isolation plays are just extensions of the dead money principle: If you can make the blinds go away, the dead money is equity to be shared between the two of you.

5. Image

There are two types of image you need to be aware of:

1. Table image
2. Self-image

1. Table image

Table image is most commonly discussed. This is the image that your opponents have of you. Do they see you as loose or tight? Wild or restrained? Do they think you always have the goods or bluff a lot? You must constantly understand what your table image is because that is what your opponents are reacting to.

Once again, there are two types of table image:

1. Evolved
2. Manufactured

1. Evolved image

"Evolved image" is how you appear based on the hands you have played, your playing frequency, and to some extent the results you have had. It is the image you generate when you simply sit at a table and play your game.

If you get a series of unplayable hands, you start to look tight. If you get a series of good playing hands, you look loose. This is especially true if you do not have to show hands down.

If you play a number of hands and win them without a showdown, opponents will begin to suspect that you must be bluffing sometimes whether you have been or not. If you get some excellent hands, raise pre-flop and have to fold before the showdown, or simply lose them all, opponents will suspect you have been raising with trash. In both cases, your table image has changed. If opponents think you are playing poor cards, regardless of the truth, you will have a hard time bluffing, but you will get called if you make value bets.

On the other hand, if you have showed down a series of very good hands that have won pots, now your opponents will show you (too much) respect. You will have evolved a solid image, whether you want one or not. Your raises are less likely to be called, as are your bluffs. However, value betting now becomes a poor proposition because if you do get called, it will be by a better hand.

Players who are unaware of their evolved image make errors.

Example 1

You have raised several pots and shown down winners. Now, you bet the river with a good hand and get raised. Unless you are certain you know how this opponent plays, he almost certainly is not bluffing. He has respect for the fact that your hands are good, and he feels he can beat a good hand.

Example 2

You have been forced to make some laydowns on the river to bets or raises, either because you were bluffing or just because you realized you were second best, your opponents may have noticed that as well. Now if you bet the river and get raised, you will have to call with any sort of decent hand, as the likelihood of someone trying to bluff you has gone way up.

Example 3

You have been raising often pre-flop and then you get three-bet, the raiser may have a much weaker hand than if this is the first raise you have made in some time.

In each instance, you need to be aware of how your evolved image has affected the range of hands your opponents will play. If you have called many hands down, you look like a calling station whether you are or not. No observant opponent will try to bluff you. If a savvy opponent bets into you, he has the goods. Don't make thin calls here.

Often, you can't help how your image evolves. Be aware at all times of how you look recently, since many opponents will credit you for playing according to that image.

2. Manufactured image

"Manufactured image" is an image you deliberately set out to create. You may select a wardrobe or accent or table mannerisms to convince your opponents you are who the manufactured image says. For example, I knew a Las Vegas pro who slept all day then went to various low-limit games dressed in a conventioneer suit with a fake plastic badge. This gave him the image of a tourist, tired from a hard day's work, who would play poorly and for fun.

Similarly, there are a number of players who have an excellent drunk act. They splash some chips for a while, making a big deal of their inability to read the board or stack chips. When they have a big hand they pounce, using their manufactured image to get excessive action. Typically, these are hit-and-run artists who leave soon after they have won a big pot, knowing their act will soon wear thin.

To some extent, *Illusion of Action* players have a combination of the two. You will need a tight table image to successfully execute situational plays, but once you have been unmasked as playing hands that most people consider unplayable, you have now manufactured a much wilder image. All further plays by your opponents must be seen in that light.

2. Self-image

Self-image is how you view yourself at the table, and how you wish to be thought of by others. Specifically, most players like to look intelligent. Poker attracts smart people because of the deep strategies and opportunities to outwit the opposition. Many smart people like to bask in the adulation of others because it makes them feel good.

You may want to explain your plays, or announce your opponent's hand that you have read, to demonstrate your intelligence and ability. Even worse, you may be tempted to tell others why the play they have just made was so poor.

 WARNING: Maintaining an image of intelligence is counter-productive to the purpose of making the most money.

In fact, you will make more money if your opponents think you are stupid. They will not give you credit for deep thinking and great strategies, and their errors mean profit for you.

The problem is that many players not only want to *be* smart, they want to *look* smart. Not only do they do things to make them look smart, they refuse to do things that may make them look stupid to some. Being an *Illusion of Action* player requires you to do some pretty stupid looking things. In fact, these are deliberate because you want the opponents to misunderstand your ability and miscalculate your plays.

You do not want to look stupid because you are stupid, but you should not mind looking foolish because you are smart enough to trick others into thinking you are stupid. Unfortunately, players whose esteem derives from others' views of them have a hard time with this concept. They really want to look smart to others. Trust me: some of the best players in the world have no fear of making silly-looking plays if they believe that is the best way to make money in the long run.

They do not go out of their way to look stupid. They are trying to win. But if they do end up with a stupid table image, they relish and attempt to reinforce it. "I am on tilt," they declare as they raise with pocket kings after just losing a bad beat. "Let's gamble," they shout as they put in an extra bet with a small pair trying to build a large multiway pot profitably. If they must fold their kings before the showdown, they don't show them around for sympathy. They extend the image by saying, "That'll teach me to raise with 5-2 suited!"

Your opponents do not want to play with a guy called "Doc". They want to play with a guy called "Nutty Barry, " who makes crazy-loose plays like raising K-3 suited and four-betting A-Q out of position. If you can play well while looking stupid, you're in a great place. Be smart after the session when you talk poker with your friends, when you post on Internet forums, and when you plot your strategy. At the table, it is fine to make silly plays as long you as you know why you are making them, and your reasons are smart ones.

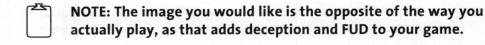 **NOTE: The image you would like is the opposite of the way you actually play, as that adds deception and FUD to your game.**

Chapter Four

Overcoming the Obstacles to Success

So far, you have learned why, how, and under what circumstances to use situational play. Unfortunately, there are several considerations that may keep you from implementing these concepts properly. Understanding them better will make it easier for you to recognize and overcome them. The issues we will explore are:

- ♠ Expanding your comfort zone
- ♠ Understanding random reinforcement
- ♠ Doing the hard work
- ♠ Tolerating volatility

Expanding your comfort zone

People play the style of game they're comfortable playing. Aggressive people play aggressively, and passive ones play passively. People who like to gamble play a gambling style, and people who like sure things play more conservatively until they make the nuts.

And many people cherry-pick the literature. They buy a bunch of poker books, then select from them the concepts that support or reinforce their comfortable position. Unfortunately for them, many books, including this one, present an integrated method in which all of the recommended plays form a complete system. Taking a concept or play out of this system may not be as effective as using it as part of the integrated whole.

For example, Doyle Brunson's classic book *Super System* presents a method for playing power no-limit hold'em in a deep-stack environment. Doyle tells us that, when he wins a pot, he always plays the next hand. Some people who read the book and do not play deep stack no-limit, or even follow any other of Doyle's principles, think that this one idea is very cool, since it validates their desire to play a lot of trash hands, and blame it on Doyle. They enjoy playing hands so they find an authority who gives them an excuse, while ignoring all of the other things they have read about tight-aggressive play because that is not how they enjoy themselves.

But playing too many hands is not the only way players fall into a comfort zone. Perhaps the most common is simply calling.

When somebody bets, it seems incredibly comfortable to call. It's a nice middle of the road, compromise action. You look at your hand and think, "Well, I don't want to fold because I may win. I don't want to raise because I may not win, and if I don't, I'll have wasted all of this money by raising. So I'll call."

That seems like a viable alternative. But it doesn't avoid a decision – it makes a decision. It makes a decision to call, but it appears like it avoids the two more drastic alternatives. By doing that, it's comfortable. Calling is comfortable.

People call before the flop when it's wrong because it is comfortable. They don't want to fold and then feel bad that they missed a chance to win a lot of money. They certainly don't want to raise because their hand is not "as good as it should be" to raise, so they call. In the middle of a hand, they call, and at the end of the hand, they call. That's an example of being comfortable.

Some people are very comfortable playing tight. It fulfils what I believe is the emotional need to avoid committing money to a pot they might lose. They first want to see if they are going to win it. Unfortunately, by waiting, they lose significant money they might be able to make by betting and raising when they are a favorite. Often, by the time they are sure they are going to win, most of their opponents are as well, and they get little or no action.

With these players, you might you get a betting pattern like this: A player makes a flush on the turn, and there's a bet, and a call and he calls. He figures another flush card might come and somebody might make a bigger flush or the board could pair and make someone a full house. He would feel bad if he raised and the opponents called and drew out on him one way or another. He wants to wait until the river to make sure his hand is good, and then he'll raise. Of course, by doing that he costs himself any number of opportunity bets.

The problem is that players like these don't fret about the bets they might have won from the other guys had they taken action; instead, they recall only the bets they lost by getting outdrawn. This pattern is common even among thoughtful players who know better. For these players the emotional desire not to lose money outweighs the rational knowledge that they should get more bets into the pot when their hand is likely best.

How about loose players? They berate themselves when they are out of a pot they would have won. They are uncomfortable when they seem to lose money by being on the sidelines. When they don't play 8-7, and the flop comes Q-8-8, and the guy with A-Q beats the guy with K-Q, then they think, "Oh, look at that pot! I would have won if only I had played 8-7." This spurs them on into playing more hands than they should, so they never get the feeling that they missed an opportunity. An old poker saying tells us, "If you play every hand to the end, you never miss a rush." Of course, you also go broke.

Players like these play so badly in part because of the emotional anguish they feel after "missing out" on a big pot. They are comfortable when they are not missing out on pots, even if they slowly drain their bankrolls a few bets at a time. When these players are advised to throw away more hands, they become very sad and can think only about the occasional pots they might have won.

Let's look at one more example: betting on the river. Very few players bet the river often enough, because something that seems scary generally hits. Even when it doesn't, they figure "the pot's big enough" and do not want to cope with a surprise raise. They think, "I can bet and probably win one more bet, but what the heck, the pot is already huge, and I don't care if I win the extra bet."

They lose track of the fact that over the course of a year every bet in every pot is the same. It doesn't matter whether you gain a bet in a two-bet pot or you gain a bet in a thirty-bet pot. (As a matter of fact, you are more likely to win that extra bet in the 30-bet pot because your opponent will call with just about anything that beats a bluff.) The absolute value of that bet is one bet. If you leave a bet on the table, it means you need to work another hour, assuming you make a bet an hour, which is the gross assumption that we make here for winning players.

This book will ask you to make plays outside your current comfort zone, making razor-thin value bets, selectively bluffing more, and raising hands with which you instinctively want to call. Perhaps in time it will become second nature, but for a while it will not be natural, and doing it will put you in other uncomfortable situations. You must be prepared to tolerate (if not embrace) these new and unusual circumstances to make more money at poker.

Understanding random reinforcement

Imagine that two of the tightest players in the world come to me for lessons. Each plays only pocket aces. They play them well, but it is the only hand they play.

I advise them to expand their game by playing pocket kings. Player A goes away and, following my advice, considerably improves his results (probably still losing, because this is not yet a winning strategy). His kings hold up most of the time, and he comes back a few weeks later for another lesson. (Guess what I will tell him.)

Player B has a different experience. The first time he raises with pocket kings, he wins the blinds. The next time, a player with A-Q calls him, and he loses when an ace comes on the turn. The next time, five players call him, and one of them stays in to make two pair. He persists and plays kings again, and another loss comes his way.

Now Player B is frustrated. He starts adding up all of the money he has lost following my (blankety-blank) advice. He decides I have no idea what I'm talking about, and goes back to just playing aces, content in the fact that he doing the right thing.

This absurdly exaggerated example illustrates a key point: poker is a very random game. You can be doing the right thing and get bad results. Conversely, you can be doing the wrong thing and get excellent results. That, coupled with the fact that poker literature contains so much contradictory advice, leaves poker students in a tough place. It is very common for students to develop a bad habit, get lucky a few times, and find some book or article that validates their bad play. Convincing them to change their approach is a difficult task.

Of course, this randomness is what makes hold'em, especially limit hold'em, such a wonderful gambling game. It's easy to learn, it has highly complex strategies, and, best of all, bad players can win often enough to convince themselves they are playing well. All of us have seen sessions in which the worst player at the table simply cannot lose a pot. If he calls three bets cold with Q-5, that is the winning hand. People (foolishly) try to tell this player how badly he is playing, but luckily, he doesn't listen. He is winning, and it is proof to him that his strategy is the right one.

Unfortunately, the same randomness that makes poker such a great gambling game makes it a difficult game to learn to play correctly. It takes both faith and discipline to continue to try a new concept long enough for it to prove itself. For some, of course, it will seem to work immediately, just like playing kings worked for Player A above. For others, it will seem to fail for a period of time.

Part of making good decisions is deciding whom to listen to and realizing that it may take a long time to develop an accurate picture of whether the new concept is working. I will work hard to earn your trust, giving you as much explanation as I can for each new concept presented in this book. I hope that I can explain these concepts clearly enough to convince you to try them in game situations. However, I ask that you understand that it may take a long time to see positive results because of the inherent randomness of the game. Please, do not lose faith quickly.

Doing the hard work

Winning poker is difficult work, and learning to win consistently is even more difficult. Many students come to me and other coaches looking for the golden road, the killer tip, or the magic key to victory. They are inevitably disappointed when I tell them they need to pay more attention, select the best games, learn how their opponents play, study betting patterns, analyze every situation, plan in advance, stay focused on the game, count the pot, compute the odds, figure out how the play might go, estimate what their opponents' think they hold and how they should respond, and then make a decision. And that's just at the table!

Away from the table they need to form study groups, write up and analyze hands, visit forums on trusted web sites, read books and magazines critically, and review their play with a trusted expert from time to time.

And there is still the emotional side of the game. They need to tolerate swings and bad beats, stay patient, not take things personally, not worry about sessions, not press, avoid tilt, and be able to put outside issues behind them at the table.

None of this is easy, and few people even come close to doing all of it. However, it illustrates how far we are from "give me a tip that will make me a winning player".

This book will improve your game by pointing out strategies and methods you may not be using or using effectively. If you can overcome the obstacles we have discussed here and are willing to do the hard work associated with learning to win big, this book will help you greatly.

Tolerating volatility

Speaking of money and discomfort, one of the most difficult changes to make is coping with the increased volatility that comes with increased profits. Most winning players have learned to play tight poker, as that is the first key to success.

However, tight play has its limitations, particularly when you play with better players at higher limits. Simply put, you don't get the action you used to get, so your profits decline. Better opponents will observe that your playing frequency is quite low and that your hand selection is predictable. They will simply avoid you when you come into a pot unless they have a premium hand as well. The money you made from what I call "the kindness of strangers" will evaporate against these better players. To make significant money you must either find worse players to play with, or vary your play enough to convince the better players to give you action somehow (much of this book tells you how).

Unfortunately, *there is no way to play less tightly without seeing some increased volatility in your results*. If you follow the strategies described in this book, you will win more and lose more, but in the end you will have a bigger net win. However, you must be fiscally and mentally prepared to handle the big swings.

Tolerating increased variance takes two things: a bankroll to handle them, and the ability to accept them. Bankroll is easy to understand – you either have it or you don't.

The psychological fortitude to accept the swings is more problematic, and it depends on the first two topics we discussed in this chapter. First, you may make changes that make you uncomfortable at the table, and second, you may not experience immediate success. Even if you are okay with the new challenges changing your game will bring, making changes and possibly losing more because of the natural swings and simply being on unfamiliar ground may be difficult.

Don't jump into the deep end if you are not a good swimmer. Take things slowly. Step down in limits and try some new things. Try only a few, at first. Keep track of your results and your overall comfort level. When you feel you understand how to play a slightly different style, go back to your old game and see what happens. Do this several times if you wish to master new concepts while not damaging your bankroll. I'm confident you will find new comfort as you overcome these obstacles.

Chapter Five

Hand Reading

Throughout this book, you will find passages telling you that your play depends on your opponents or on your read. Therefore, it makes sense to spend a bit of time discussing hand reading.

Top professionals' proficiency at hand reading accounts for a large part of their edge over average players. The better you can become at solving the puzzle of what your opponent holds, the more money you will make. In fact, the ability to read hands is the gateway skill to expert play.

Hand reading always considers all of the hands your opponent might hold for his actions. Based on this, you strive to narrow down the number by logic, or you try to take the action that makes the most sense with the understanding that any action may fail even if all of your logic is correct.

Example

To take a simple example, assume you have two queens. A tight player raises in early position before the flop. Obviously, he could have two aces, in which case you should fold. But he also could have K-K, Q-Q, J-J, A-K or A-Q, and in the case of some players, A-J, K-Q or even 10-10. On balance, you should reraise even though it could be the wrong play if he holds exactly the top of his range.

Notice this is very different from simply putting him on A-K. As the hand progresses, you will work to narrow down the likely hands based on his future actions, including his reaction to your three-bet.

Hand Reading Elements

Let's consider these. You need to understand:

- ♠ How well your opponent plays.
- ♠ How he approaches the game (how he thinks).
- ♠ His frame of mind.
- ♠ What he thinks about how you play.
- ♠ His tells.

That's an awful lot of knowledge about your opponent you need before you can start determining what your opponent holds.

In addition, you need to understand and apply math to certain situations, so we will discuss that as well.

How well your opponent plays

Poker thought occurs at many levels. Perhaps the biggest challenge in accurate hand reading is the assessment of your opponent's level. The better your opponent plays, the more logical and therefore predictable his play becomes. Of course, the better he plays, the more he understands how important it is to vary his game to try to deceive you as well, but in many circumstances his play will be straightforward. If he plays terribly, he might have anything, and you will have to do more guessing than analysis. Happily, if he plays terribly, you will get his money eventually because of the many errors he will make.

As a rule of thumb, the bigger the pot, the more straightforward the play, particularly on the turn and river. Obviously this is not always true, but players tend to be quite honest on the turn on large, multiway pots that are clearly going to a showdown. In smaller pots, or heads-up situations, you can't rely on much of anything.

How he approaches the game

Beyond his level of thought, you also need to know his general approach. Does he like to bet draws, or only made hands? Does he bluff raise? Will he bet the river for value with a marginal hand or only with a very good one? Does he three-bet the flop with top pair, or must he have a better holding? If he has K-K and an ace is on the board, will he call all the way down, fold early, or try a raise? You must study each opponent, as your knowledge of his approach will determine what hands you think he will play in a given situation.

His frame of mind

Not being a robot, your opponent has moods. He acts differently when winning than when losing. He might play differently early in the session than he does later, or when getting ready to leave. He might get upset by a bad beat, or be enjoying a great joke. All of these moods affect his decision process, and you must take them into account when you determine how he might play a hand. One that he may play cautiously early he may play boldly after winning a few pots. The better you understand this, the more accurate your reads will be.

What he thinks about how you play

While you try to solve him, he could be working on you as well. Depending on his opinion and how well he plays and adjusts, his responses to you could be vastly different from how he plays others. If you see him three-betting with A-J, it might be because a loose player has raised in late position. It does not necessarily mean he would three-bet you with the same hand. In fact, if he thinks you are much tighter, he might have thrown away the A-J if you had raised. You must understand this or else you could include A-J in the hands you believe he could hold when he three-bets you and be entirely incorrect.

His tells

Chapter 6 covers typical tells you can look for. In general, your opponents' physical actions and reactions must enter into your assessment of their holdings. To the astute observer, a typical player's hand, eye, face, and body movements provide significant insight into his holdings. Even if much of the time you can't find a tell, you should still keep focused on this area during live play, as you will discover more and more. When you do spot one, the value is considerable.

Math

Only rarely can you narrow down your opponent's holding to a specific hand. More often, you will narrow his holdings down to a few. You can then use math to determine the likelihood of each holding, and the pot odds to determine the consequences of each of your possible actions based on these probabilities. Just because a hand is more likely does not mean you should act as if he held it.

Example

On the river, you hold A♣-Q♣ and board is 2♣-3♦-6♣-7♥-Q♦. Your opponent, who has been representing a big hand, bets the river. You decide his only likely holdings are A-A, K-K, Q-Q, or A-K. Given the board and your hand, there are three ways he can hold A-A, six ways he can hold K-K, one way he can have Q-Q, and 12 ways he can have A-K. Thus, the odds are 12-to-10 that you have him beat. Does this mean you should raise? Of course not, since if he has A-K he can't call, and if he has anything else, you will lose an extra bet (at least).

Actually, I fudged, because the problem is more complex than this. The math regarding his holding is correct as far as it goes. But the question to ask yourself is how often will he actually bet each of these hands on the river. It's true you are a 12-to-10 favorite against his holdings, but not necessarily against his bettable holdings. If he is the type to bet every hand to the end, the math holds and you must call. If he would never bet his A-K here, you can't beat anything and must fold. This latter may be closer to the case. If there are four or more big bets in the pot including his river bet, the question you have to ask is, "Will this guy bet A-K as much as 25% of the time?" If he will, then you will lose 10 times for every three you win (25% of the 12 times he holds A-K), giving you a price of

3/13 or around 23%. If you believe he will bet an A-K as much as 25% of the time he has one, call if the pot is offering 4-to-1 or greater.

Generally, of course, you will not know, but you must make a decision based on whatever clues you can muster. Even if you are right about his betting frequency, you will be correct to call but still lose the bet and the pot slightly more than three-quarters of the time.

Common errors

You can always make an error in reading hands, but some errors are very common. These include:

- ♠ Putting someone on a hand.
- ♠ Staying with your read.
- ♠ Thinking the other guy plays like you.

Putting someone on a hand

Many players confuse hand reading with the concept of putting a person on a hand. For example, you raise pre-flop and someone three-bets. You have seen this player three-bet with small pairs, so you decide to put him on a small pair. This is not hand reading – this is guessing or hoping. He could have a small pair, big pair, big cards, or be making a weird play. You need to think about all of these options and narrow them down during the rest of the hand. If you simply put a player on a hand, you preclude considering other options.

Staying with your read

This error is closely related to the last one. In this case, you put together clues and decide what a likely set of hands is. Then out of the blue comes a totally unexpected bet or raise. You must stop right here and reassess, but many players don't. They just plow ahead with their previous read, frequently making a disastrous reraise and losing several extra bets.

Thinking the other guy plays like you

You know how you play, but that does not mean the other player agrees with your theories of the game. I have seen loose players call down a super-tight player because the caller would occasionally bluff in the situation. Sure, but the opponent would never think of it. Just because you would never call a raise with A-3 offsuit doesn't mean the other guy won't. You must be able to allow for the poor plays of the other guy, and not just pay off and complain because "he can't have that hand."

Now that we have covered the basics of hand reading, let's try a real life example.

A practice hand

You hold A♠-K♠. The player on your right is a cautious professional, who plays well but unimaginatively. He thinks you are a tough professional who is hard to read. Your opponent raises before the flop, you three-bet, and he calls after everyone else folds. On the flop of Q♣-7♠-4♠, he checks, you bet, and he calls. He bets out when he sees the A♦ hit the turn. You raise, and he calls. On the river, the 7♥ does not help you. He checks. What hand(s) could he hold and how should you continue? Really try to decide before you read on.

OK, time's up. I hope you said he has A-K, as that is certainly his most likely holding. He raised before the flop and almost certainly has a big pair or a big ace. With a pair smaller than queens, he might check-call the flop, but his turn play makes no sense. With A-J, he should not have called the flop, and should not have called your raise on the turn. With A-Q, he would have done more raising either on the flop or on the turn. With A-A or K-K he probably would have reraised pre-flop or put more action in on the flop. Certainly with A-A he would be three-betting the turn. With K-K, even if he called the flop and bet the turn (unlikely) he would have folded for the raise. So he has A-K, or else has suddenly morphed into a much trickier player than you thought.

What should you do on the river? Even though I love betting the river, I think this is an easy check. He almost certainly has A-K and you are chopping once you missed your spade freeroll. If your read is wrong, it is far more likely that you are somehow beat than that you would win an extra bet. Check and chop gets my vote.

Conclusion

Hand reading is difficult, part skill and part art. It requires extensive effort, a very good memory, and intense concentration. Once you start mastering it, though, reads become more automatic and improve over time. You will still make errors through incorrect reads, and you will have many hands where reads are not possible. But overall, your results will improve dramatically once you begin to really buckle down and start reading hands instead of "putting someone on a hand".

Chapter Six

Tells

I have always found it much easier to beat people I can see. My win rate in live play is better than it is on the Internet. One key reason is that live opponents offer numerous tells.

Some players say that tell play is overrated, and perhaps it is. Observing betting patterns will gain you far more knowledge of your opponents' habits and holdings than watching their breathing patterns. Nevertheless, an opponent's demeanor, attitude, posture, movements, and appearance can provide information that will win or save you money.

Reading opponents is a key part of situational play. The more you know about the enemy, the better you can assess and optimize the current situation. Most of your knowledge will come from watching how they have played their cards on previous deals, but specific situational knowledge can also come from reading tells.

I will cover some tells that I use, including some that are not that well covered in the literature[5]. We will discuss this topic in three parts:

- ♠ Opponents' tells
- ♠ Inducing tells
- ♠ Your tells

---

[5] The literature I have seen and used include *The Book of Tells* by Mike Caro, and *Read' Em and Reap* by Joe Navarro.

Opponents' tells

Opponents offer many tells. For discussion, I have divided them into categories:

1. Appearance tells
2. Demeanor tells
3. Movement tells
4. Verbal tells
5. Fake tells

1. Appearance tells

Stereotypes work. That's why they become stereotypes. They don't always work because people are individuals, but if you have little to go on, trust stereotypes until you see evidence to the contrary.

Because most of them are well known, I will not go into detail. For example, everyone understands that "The older the player, the higher the kicker," is generally true. Some young players are very tight, but most can't resist the temptation to mix it up, make action raises, steal with any two, and execute other highly aggressive plays. Some oldsters play this way too, but most have learned the "value of value" and wait for hands they know are proven +EV or better.

Clothes make the man. Meticulous dressers tend to play conservatively. Players who don't much care how they look frequently are less cautious about how they play. This tends to apply more to men than women, because most women dress nicely and with care regardless of how they play.

Look at accessories, particularly wristwatches. People who wear watches that cost more than 10 racks of chips are far more likely to call a river bet than players with watches that cost far less than a buy-in. Jewellery would be a similarly reliable tell if you could do appraisals on the spot.

I am often asked about "TV players". These guys wear sunglasses at the table, have huge earphones, and baseball caps. Many of these players play a TV game of hyper-aggressive bets and raises. Contrarily, others play a totally locked down game, only entering with premium holdings and playing solidly thereafter. Only rarely do you see a TV player play an average game.

Here is the real reason TV players wear the sunglasses, hats, and shirts that cover their bodies. The two observable reflex responses that humans cannot control are pupillary dilation and adrenalin. At times of excitement, or if one sees something wonderful, the pupils dilate. Some top players watch for this, and use it as a tell. Sunglasses and wide brimmed hats block opponents' ability to see this response. Similarly, adrenalin produces rapid pulse rate, which in some people can be observed in the neck or forearm. Some players believe others can see this response and wear clothing to cover any area that might give this pulse beat increase away.

Earphones rarely have any tell significance. Once in a while, you will see a player with a big hand turn down the volume on his music player. Most earphone users wear them to enhance concentration and often record their own affirmations to help while playing. ("You are playing well." "Stay in the moment." "Pause before responding to raises.") Others actually keep the volume off so they can hear everything that is said, but pretend to be listening to something so they do not have to respond or engage in conversation.

2. Demeanor tells

Look at how comfortable people are. I have changed games because several players in my game were too comfortable, feeling too secure in the cardroom element.

I do not mean just identifying novices, though that helps. I mean players who have no tension about their plays or results. People who can take everything in stride, who do not get a little upset about beats, who don't agonize over the occasional decision, and who pay attention effortlessly are dangerous. You must distinguish them from players who are just there for a good time and don't care much about their surroundings. The former are watching the game; the latter are watching everything but the game.

Players sitting straight up are more interested in playing a hand than slouching players, who frequently are sitting that way because they are waiting patiently for a good hand. On average, a resting player who plays a hand starts with better cards than an attentive person. Resting players are relaxing and not anxious to play a hand. When they do decide to arouse themselves to play a hand, they are not just mixing it up or having fun – they have quality cards. Slouching players who suddenly sit up are the most dangerous.

One really useful playing tell in this category is observing players as they see the turn and river cards. First, remember always to watch your opponent when the dealer is exposing the board. If you have more than one, pick the one who tends to give you the most information, the weakest player, or the one on your left who will play after you.

This suggestion follows the general principle that you should never look at anything that is not going to change until you must do so. Occasionally, an opponent with a draw looks at the turn or river cards with a sense of urgency that is not there when he has made his hand already. You can sometimes surmise that he was drawing and missed whether or not he registers disappointment when he misses. Of course, some people give extremely clear tells that they have missed. Since they are planning to fold, they no longer care about the hand and are not concerned about the information they give away.

Finally, look out for what I call the "Aces Glaze". Some players, when they have pocket aces, act almost as if mesmerized. They bet when it is their turn regardless of the board or action, as if an invisible force were driving them to bet. These actions tend to be accompanied by a distant eye expression, which seems to say, "I have aces. I must play this hand to the end regardless, so I do not need to look or think." There is no other hand that people play in this fashion.

3. Movement tells

These are what most people mean when they talk about tells. They envision some twitch or other motion that a player makes when he is bluffing or holding a huge hand. I suppose such things exist outside of movies, but I rarely see them.

Instead, I rely on more subtle repetitive movements. Here is the key:

 TIP: Look for differences

One movement is not much, but a different movement may mean something. If an opponent usually bets by cutting his chips, but later bets by just putting them down in a tower, there may be a meaning. The meaning depends on what sorts of hands the player showed when doing the cutting motion.

If you play a 4-chip, 8-chip game, watch for this tell on the turn or river. You bet the turn and player sitting with normal 20-chip stacks removes the top four chips and then pushes out the 16-chip tower to make a raise. This is usually a very confident move, as his hand is so big that he has time to think about clever ways to put his chips in the pot.

Watch players on your left after the cards are dealt. Most opponents are savvy enough to not hold their cards in the wrist-cocked mucking position when they are folding, but some do, especially before the flop because they have lost interest in the hand. Look for a difference: Is the wrist cocked some times and not others?

Many moves are harder to spot. Perhaps your opponent leaves his cards in his right hand after looking if he is going to fold, but quietly shifts them to his left (so he can put chips in with his right) if he is planning to play. This is an unaware tell, but very useful in our positional game. For every opponent you can see planning to fold behind you, you can promote your position one place.

Many players watch for facial tells, but they are not that easy to spot. I focus on hand tells, because they are far more plentiful and easier to read. As before, no particular hand movement is meaningful, but if a player holds his cards one way this time and another way later, or bets one way and then another, you should try to solve the puzzle.

Checking is also interesting. Many players check many different ways. Sometimes an opponent who is planning to check-raise the turn does an elaborate check on the flop and the same elaborate check on the turn. He hopes you noticed his check on the flop was followed by a call, so the exact same check motion will not frighten you on the turn. If that was not the way he had been checking when he had no interest in the pot, be very afraid.

Tempo is well worth watching. One particular tempo tell you can often spot is the quick, almost thought-free cold call of a raise on the flop. It almost always indicates a flush draw if this is present, and trips if the board is paired. The idea is that after a bet and raise, most people need to stop and think, at least for a moment, about how to proceed. But players with a flush draw already understand they will be calling all raises to the river, so there is nothing to think about. Similarly, if a player flops trips (not a set) and decides to raise on the turn, as many do, they already know they will be calling whatever comes their way on the flop. They "smooth call" with no concern.

As the action is coming to a player in a multiway pot, he sometimes prepares to respond before it is actually his turn. He may move his cards, look back at his hand, organize some chips, or simply make small gestures that you can eventually read. Many of these are unaware actions because he assumes you are looking at the bettor and not at him. A few players have developed a habit of keeping their hands off the table except when it is their turn. I dislike playing with them, because they remove one of my advantages.

Players who do chip riffles and other tricks sometimes stop or do something different with their hands under pressure. Particularly on the river, after they bet, they may do one thing with a strong hand (like keep riffling) and another with a marginal hand or bluff (like stop riffling). They may do the opposite. Again, if there are different actions by the same person, try to figure out when they do which one.

4. Verbal tells

Some players just yak and yak. They have a verbal patter designed to confuse you. "Please don't call." "I think I have you this time." "Raise it and take it." "Can you beat two queens?" They go on and on.

If you spend time listening to this and trying to decipher it, you will generally fail. They have usually perfected their chatter, and the time you spend concentrating on it is worse than wasted; it is time you could have been thinking about something productive.

On the other hand, some players rarely speak. When they do, they frequently tell the truth and hope you think they are lying. In my experience, when they answer a question, players who are generally quiet tell the truth or refuse to answer. This has proven valid over 80% of the time. I know this is anecdotal and not scientific, and it may change if people read this, but that's the way I have seen people act.

5. Fake tells

Opponents also know about tells, and are happy to throw false ones at you from time to time. Here is one such experience that happened to me.

Many years ago, I was at a $20-$40 table. A player two to my right bet the river. I hesitated, trying to decide whether to make a close call. He picked his hand off the table to show it to the two onlookers behind him.

This is a classic tell. People with bad hands and bluffs do not show them proudly to onlookers. If they win, they want to pretend they had a good hand in front of their friends. So I released my hand.

As I was releasing, one of the onlookers said, "Nice hand." This was a certain tell that the enemy was bluffing, and one of the dangers of showing your hand to friends. The friend was foolishly trying to promote the bluff by helping out. No way he would ever say that if he was looking at a nice hand. I nearly broke my wrist diving across the table to retrieve my hand, but to no avail. I had folded and the bad guy won the pot.

Inducing tells

Sometimes, you can gain information by actively inducing it. Remarkably, one of the easiest ways to get information is to ask for it.

 TIP: Talk to the players. Ask questions.

First, this is the friendly thing to do, and it's more fun than just sitting there like a puma in the tall weeds waiting to pounce. Second, players will tell you things that may help. How are they feeling? How high do they generally play? If they are from out of town, where do they play? What do they do for a living? How long have they been at the table? Are they winning or losing for this trip or session?

One question many players are happy to discuss is, "Why did you play the hand that way?" They play because they enjoy the strategic aspects of the game, and delight in explaining their theories to others. Often, they will launch into lengthy reviews of their play, including alternatives considered and rejected. Whether they are right or wrong, they are telling you their philosophy of the game. You can learn things that will help you in future play against them. On occasion, I will learn something that helps improve my game as well.

You can also play in such a way that you can induce tells. For example, you can bet into someone who raised before the flop. He is expecting you to check to him, and is ready to bet because that is what most pre-flop raisers do. Betting into him forces him to make a decision he may not have been prepared to make, and his response can give you information about the strength of his holding.

Your tells

The easiest player to keep track of is you, yet few players really monitor themselves. Try to play tell-free poker. Notice what you do with your hands, your bets, your eyes, your posture, and your words when you are happy, sad, bluffing, hoping for a call, or drawing.

When I was starting out at $3-$6, I noticed that I could not control my betting speed. If I had a good hand I would bet with a nice tempo, but if I was bluffing, I would bet quickly. This was not conscious, but I saw it happening too often.

I took home a stack of chips and practiced betting on my kitchen table. I developed a smooth slide-and-cut motion I thought I could repeat every time, bluffing or not. This muscle memory training helped my confidence as well as giving me a better chance to play tell-free.

If you are not sure, ask a friend to watch you play. He can observe some unconscious movements or behaviors that you can address.

Work to avoid the common look-back-to-see-what-suits-you-have tell. This tell commonly happens when three suited cards appear on the board, either on the flop or on the turn. A player who has suited cards knows it. A player with offsuit cards needs to look back to see if he has a flush draw. Avoid this by remembering what suits you hold. Here is a chart with all six combinations and names for them:

Suits	Name
Clubs and Spades	Black
Diamonds and Hearts	Red
Clubs and Diamonds	Low (first in alphabetical order)
Hearts and Spades	High (last in alphabetical order)
Clubs and Hearts	Round (tops of the pips)
Diamonds and Spades	Pointed (tops of the pips)

Should you fake a tell? I don't recommend it. I strongly encourage you to play tell-free poker. When you flash fake tells, you play mind games that you may win or lose. Playing with no tells permanently reduces your opponents' edge.

Finally, I have seen players proudly announce their opponents' tell. This is yet another "look how smart I am" play which is extremely stupid. If you know an opponent holds his chips a certain way when he does not want to you to bet, and you bet and he folds, the last thing you should do is explain why you bet. Why would you want to inform your opponents of this tell, or worse, let the offender know about it? Wouldn't you want to use it again? Yet, I have seen well-known players do this. They let their ego become more important than the money.

Conclusion

If you have to focus on one thing at the table, let it be how your opponents play. People play in reliable patterns, and if you make the effort to learn them, you will have a good idea of the cards your opponents hold.

Tells are less reliable, and harder to hone in on. However, adding tell play to your arsenal will increase your ability to read situations to your benefit. The more you watch, the more you will see, and the better you will become.

Chapter Seven

Raise or Fold Situations

One of the most confusing things for me to grasp as a beginning player was the concept of "raise or fold" situations. It seemed to me that if you could raise or fold, then surely calling would be a terrific compromise. I was always a compromising sort of person.

I have since learned to think of the situation as similar to deciding what to do on a busy street. You can drive east, or you can drive west. Parking in the center is not a useful compromise. In fact, it is likely to get you hurt.

Despite being an extremely imperfect analogy, it helps me focus on the concept. And the concept explains why you will see so many players who you respect doing a lot more raising or folding than calling.

Certainly, calling has a significant place in poker. So I will try here to define how to recognize at least the most common raise or fold situations. The specific criteria are:

♠ **The pot must be multiway.** There are no raise or fold situations in heads-up hands. With no players to act behind you, you can select from any action you feel will give you the best chance. For example, if you feel your opponent is bluffing in a heads-up situation, you can simply call and hope he bluffs off some more money. With other players drawing to beat you in the hand, you cannot simply play the bluffer, but must raise to reduce the odds for the drawing players.

♠ **There must be a bet before you**. (Obviously, you could not raise or fold unless there is a bet, but I like to be comprehensive.)

♠ **There must be no intervening callers.** You are next to act after the bet. If there is an intervening caller, and you feel all of the other criteria are met, you still might decide this is raise or fold, but it is not mandatory.

♠ **You must believe you have the best hand, or are choosing to represent the best hand.** If you have a draw, raising reduces your pot odds both by having you put more money in the pot and by eliminating some players that could help to increase your odds. If instead you believe you have or may have the best hand, raising helps eliminate players who may be drawing to beat you, or charges them the maximum to try to outdraw you.

♠ **There must be players behind you who could improve to make hands that could beat yours**. If you hold an unbeatable hand, there is no requirement to raise (and folding would be a really bad idea).

The general concept here is, if there is a bet and you hold (or want to represent) a made hand, you do not want to call if your made hand is second best, particularly as there may still be raises behind you. You would be out of position with respect to the rest of the field, and thus need to play more tightly.

On the other hand, if you do feel your hand might be best, then calling simply invites people to trail along inexpensively to try to beat you.

This concept sometimes requires some fine judgment on your part, but if you think of these situations in the terms I set out, your judgment will improve. You will be folding more and therefore seeing some pots you might have won go to other people, but you will be saving money in the long run.

Let's look at some examples.

Example 1

You raise pre-flop with A♠-J♥ from middle position. The cutoff, button and big blind all call, putting 8½ small bets in the pot. These are typical players and call raises somewhat too loosely, but the two behind you would three-bet with premium hands. The flop is K♦-J♣-5♥, giving you middle pair and top kicker. The big blind bets. What do you do?

Because you are in this chapter, you know you must raise or fold. If you have a second-best hand, calling is silly as you are not getting a price to draw and you would be pricing in the players behind you if they have gutshot draws like A-10 and Q-9. And you may get raised behind you, and your relative position is suddenly quite poor. If the big blind would bet draws and second pair here, you may easily have the best hand and should raise.

Your decision depends on how the big blind plays. If he had a king, would he bet out or check, hope you bet, and try to check-raise the field? If he would bet hands weaker than a king, then raise him, hope to drive out the remainder of the opponents, and try to figure out later whether you are ahead or behind. If he would primarily bet a king here, fold. Many opponents who might bet a number of hands heads-up will only bet a king or better into a large field like this, so you must consider that as well.

Of course, many decisions are easier than this. If you had A-K, your raise would be easy. If you had 8-8, you would fold. Marginal hands for this situation like Q-Q or J-10 call for finer judgments. In multiway pots, if you are undecided, you should fold. Just remember: calling is the worst option of all.

Example 2

This is a more complex example from a Bellagio $30-60 game. I got a free play in the big blind holding K♠-7♣. Four players had limped, and the small blind had called, so we were looking at six small bets.

The flop came K♣-10♦-3♠, and the small blind checked. This is not the sort of situation I like to get involved with. I had a hand I would never have played had it not been in the blind. I was out of position. My kicker was weak. The pot was small. If I bet and got any action, there was a good chance I was beat. Generally, my plan in this sort of circumstance is to check and fold if there is action, though I will check-raise an aggressive button player if everyone checks to him and he bets. I decided to do that here.

Somewhat surprisingly, it was checked around. The presence of the ten made it very unlikely that anyone else held a king, because it would have been too dangerous to give a free card to the various draws that are frequently present when two Broadway cards are on the flop. It was even unlikely, for much the same reasons, that any of the last players to act had as much as a ten since they probably would bet that. It was starting to look like my weak free hand was good.

The turn bought the 2♦ and the small blind checked. I had definite reason to believe I had the best hand. In addition, since a lot of players will bluff at a pot from the blind after everyone has checked the flop, there was a good chance I might get action from a suspicious second-best hand. I bet out, fully expecting to get either zero or one caller. After all, the pot was small, my bet was one-third of the pot, and nobody had shown any strength on the somewhat dangerous flop.

Unexpectedly, an action-fest broke out. The bearded guy on my left called, the college-looking kid to his left called and, after a fold, the guy wearing the purple shirt raised! What was going on here?

The small blind folded, and it was up to me again. I did not mind the calls so much, but the raise really made me pause for thought. There was some chance purple-shirt had just made a set of deuces, or that he had been (incorrectly) slowplaying some form of large hand on the flop. If that was the case, I was in deep trouble, and possibly drawing dead.

On the other hand, I had seen him make a number of strange raises earlier in the session. This could be another creative offering from his somewhat bizarre decision-making apparatus, and I could easily be ahead. I was also influenced by the fact that he was slumped in his chair. Many players with really big hands sit up and look interested.

It occurred to me that I was looking at a classical raise or fold situation. There was a bet to me (a raise, but still a single new bet to deal with), there were no intervening players, there were players to act behind me, and they were almost certainly drawing to beat me. If I decided I likely had the best hand, I needed to protect it. If I was in trouble, I should get away from the hand now.

I decided purple-shirt was unpredictable enough that I had to play my hand for the best one at this point, subject to changing my mind later if the action dictated. That being the case, though, I had to raise. So indeed I three-bet here, not really knowing what to expect. The bearded guy called two more big bets, the college guy folded, and purple-shirt just called. That was a relief. If he had raised again, I might have had to release my hand even though the pot had now grown quite large.

The river was the 3♣. This seemed safe in terms of draws, anyway. But I had to decide whether to bet. It seemed clear that the bearded guy was on a draw and had missed. That left unpredictable purple-shirt. I certainly did not want to face a raise since I still had a suspect hand, in spite of my bravado in three-betting the previous street. Plus, a check by me could possibly induce a bluff. Since I determined that I had more to gain by checking than by betting, I checked. So did everyone else. I showed down my king-rag and it was good. The bearded guy showed me Q♦-9♦, so he had a flush draw with a gutshot straight draw as well. Purple-shirt just mucked and slumped a bit more.

I thought this was a most unusual hand. I had checked the

flop, three-bet the turn, and checked the river. I do not recall ever seeing a hand like that before. Also, my assessment of the somewhat unusual raise or fold situation had been correct. I was faced with such a situation, even though it came after a raise rather than a bet, and fortunately I had made the right decision.

Conclusion

Raise or fold situations occur frequently, including before the flop. Every time someone bets and you are next to act, consider whether you are facing such a situation. If you are, you must become willing to act decisively.

For many, this represents a considerable expansion of their comfort zone. Remember, calling when facing a raise or fold condition is akin to standing in the middle of the street because you can't decide whether to go left or right. Just because you take a middle position doesn't make you any safer. It just means you can get into trouble from both sides (in the poker case, the player betting into you and the ones left to act).

I am no longer a compromising sort of person in these situations, considerably improving my results. You can improve yours as well by recognizing these raise or fold opportunities, and acting appropriately.

Chapter Eight

Making One Big Bet per Hour

Conventional wisdom states that the goal of live cash game players is one big bet per hour. The reality is, of course, that it's just a number. Some professional players make more than that, sometimes as much a two big bets per hour. Most make less, and still support themselves.

They make that money simply by playing a lot of hours. A tight $20-$40 pro who can bring home $25-$30 per hour can make between $50,000 and $90,000 per year, depending on luck and hours played.

For our purposes, we want to look at those select pros who actually do generate 1+ BB/hr at $30-$60 and up, and examine some of the ways they do it. Much of what they do involves "soft skills", such as game selection and mental preparation. Since this is a strategy book, we will look at the strategic techniques they use to generate income.

I am presenting these methods in a rough hierarchy of skills. As you move from easy games to tougher games – as you start to meet more skilful opponents – you need to develop new skills if you wish to continue to win. As you develop these new skills, you will also need to reduce your dependence on your previous skills.

Let me try a slightly tortured analogy. As a young Little League pitcher, a kid may develop a terrific fastball. It may terrorize his youthful opponents, and he may progress rapidly. But as he advances, he will come across hitters who can hit fastballs. If they couldn't, *they* could not have advanced. If our kid wants to go to the next level, he will need to develop new skills, like a curveball, slider, or change-up. He will use the fastball less and less. Again, as he moves through the minors, he will continually need to improve his speed, variety, and location, or he will be left behind by those who do. As the opponents get tougher, he must continue to add and grow. As he does, his reliance on the fastball diminishes.

A similar evolution of skills happens in poker. A player may start out playing tight, and win against loose opponents. If he tries to move up to more advanced games, he finds that everyone can play selectively, and he needs to add skills to continue to win. The skills in this article are (roughly) in the order that professionals develop them. Certainly many paths are available, but to reach one big bet per hour in tough middle-limit or higher games, pros must not only develop most or all of the skills, but do so in approximately this order. They then choose to utilize the skills best suited for the particular game they find themselves in.

In general, the skills they use are:

1. Playing tight
2. Folding early
3. Reading hands
4. Avoiding traps
5. Winning without the best hand
6. Inducing calls and bluffs
7. Playing the players

1. Playing tight

We all understand playing tight. You just do not play many hands, reserving all of your action for the few premium hands you receive. This method is in itself sufficient to beat almost every low-limit game. Enough players are making enough errors, playing too many hands and playing them far too long, that the tight player simply out-waits and out-powers them on the hands he does play. By always starting with the best hand against opponents who play too many mediocre hands, the player can generate a decent winning rate.

Does it work? Take a look at the pros playing in $4-$8 games, for example. They make between $6-$10 an hour, in general, simply by being tighter than anyone else in the game. These pros play as many hours as necessary to pay for rent, transportation, and food. It is not a very glamorous life, to be sure, but many value the lifestyle and freedom.

I call this form of professional play "relying on the kindness of strangers". The pros are doing nothing special, except to hope they find lots of bad opponents. This approach works well, to some degree or another, at the low limits up to around $6-$12. Beyond that, opponents improve to the point where just playing tight may win, but not at that elusive 1 BB/hr rate. My estimate is that tight but unimaginative play will get you around $10-$20/hr in most $15-$30 games. Play higher limits than that, and you need considerably more weapons just to get above breaking even, much less to the 1 BB/hr plateau.

2. Folding early

You might think this sounds a lot like playing tight, but it is really different. Many tight players simply cannot let go of a hand. They figure that they have waited so long to get a premium hand that they might as well play it to the river. Frequently they make what I call "sympathy calls". They get pocket kings, bet or call all the way into an ace on the board, lose to some weak player who called a pre-flop raise with an A-3 offsuit, then show their cowboys around so everyone can see how unfair life is.

Well, aces beat kings no matter how good a player you are or how long you waited for the kings to show up. Pros let the hand go quickly almost all of the time. In fact, pros let a lot of hands go that many other players invest in.

 TIP: A significant piece of that 1 BB/hr comes from the money pros do *not* put into the pot and do not eventually lose.

Another example occurs when a player hits a small piece of the flop. Average players stay in far too long with minor holdings, hoping to hit a kicker, second pair, or runner-runner draw. Successful players abandon these hands right away unless the odds are significantly in their favor.

If you sit around low- and middle-limit games and listen to the table talk, you will hear a lot of players saying things like: "I know you have me beat, but I have to call." "I had to call her, I had pocket aces." By contrast, when you listen to winning players and pros talk, the conversation centers on, "How could I have gotten off that hand? I can't believe I paid him off; I must be slipping." Their focus is on saving bets, not on winning pots offering poor odds. Hey, if you can save 1 BB/hr, and you were breaking even before, you have achieved your goal without having to win anything new.

Playing at this level, pros respect most raises, give up big pairs they feel are beaten, give up on what might be second-best kickers early, and do not buck the odds to make draws. You can, too.

A quick word of caution is in order. It is possible to abandon too many hands in aggressive games.

Example

Assume you raise with 8♣-8♠ in the power position, and are called by the button and big blind. The flop is Q♠-9♥-6♥. The big blind checks and later folds after you bet and the button raises. Is this the time to surrender? Maybe if the button is a straightforward player, but in aggressive middle-limit and higher games, he could have J-10, K-J, hearts, A-6, 5-5, and many other hands you can beat. Granted this is a tough situation of the type you will face daily in strong games, but if you simply abandon the hand every time, your opponents will raise you to death.

You have to vary your play here by folding, reraising, and calling and betting the turn if a seeming blank comes. You might even consider calling the raise and check-raising the turn if an offsuit seven or five hits, giving you some form of straight draw. You will win some and lose some, but justifying folding every time because you fold fast will eventually cost you too much. Knowledge of the opponent will help you make the best decision, and you may still chose to fold the majority of the time. Eventually, though, you will have to show opponents they cannot simply raise you off everything but top pair or better.

Example

In counterpoint, here is a good quick fold. You hold A♦-K♥ and raise from early position. A middle player, the cutoff, the button, and the big blind call. The flop is 9♠-8♣-3♦. The big blind bets. You getting 11-to-1 and should fold anyway. You clearly have to improve to win, as you are not going to the river hoping A-K is good. You have no clean outs, as any ace or king could give someone two pair if they do not have it already. Any of the remaining opponents can raise, either because they have a good hand or a good draw, and a three-bet is certainly possible. You missed, your prospects are poor, you are in a raise or fold situation, and fold should be an easy option.

I held this hand recently, and folded. The player behind me called with A-J, hit his jack, and lost several bets when the big blind showed him a set of threes. This kind of fast fold keeps you from bleeding away chips hand after hand and night after night.

3. Reading hands

Once you get past really soft games and into middle-limits, fewer players play terribly. Simply playing tight and folding hands early will not be enough to get the money. In these tougher games all successful players must become at least very good at reading hands.

Poker would be an easier (if very silly) game if all of the cards were dealt face up. Pros work very hard at trying to achieve the next best thing: figuring out their opponents' holdings based on their actions and tendencies. In reality, though it happens occasionally, most pros cannot specify a holding exactly. Putting an opponent on a range of hands, figuring the probabilities of each, and acting accordingly is normally the best one can do.

So how do you do it? Chapter 5 covers the parameters you need to use in reading hands. The most important factor of course, is opponents' tendencies. Which ones are loose and which ones are tight? Who is clever and who is clueless? Who bets draws and who bets only made hands? Does this opponent play "by the book", or is she creative?

You need to look at all of the showdowns, then go back and reconstruct the betting. Did this opponent three-bet pre-flop with pocket fives? Many opponents will never do it, but if this one will, you need to make a note of it. Did this opponent have a chance to raise on the turn with the nuts and not do it? You need to know who may be capable of doing that.

Who in your game bluffs, and who probably has not bluffed in years? Who will try to steal blinds with nothing, and who needs real values? If you bet into an ace, and your opponent has one, will he raise?

Acting on all of this information, you should try to build a picture.

Example

Take a five-way unraised pot. You see a flop of K♥-J♠-5♠. The small blind bets and the big blind calls. If the big blind is a good player, you can be pretty sure he does not have a king, but rather is on a draw. Do you see why? If he had a king, he would be anxious to raise, and eliminate players who may have smaller pairs or gutshot draws. But with a draw, he would want to invite a multiway pot to get the best pot odds if he does make his hand. Using this preliminary read, you begin to build up a picture of this and the other holdings around the table. Of course, you can be wrong (he might have decided to slowplay a set of jacks), and you need to be ready to take in contradictory information and resolve it. Your read makes an excellent beginning to your decisions regarding how (or if) to play, or whether to pay off if a draw gets there.

The more you try to read hands, and the closer you can come, the more successful you will be. Of course, you need to couple this detective work with taking appropriate and consistent action.

4. Avoiding traps

Poker traps come in an enormous number of situations, and nobody avoids them all. I will point out a few here that seem to repeat often.

Your aggressive opponent raises before the flop and gets a couple of callers. After the flop, they check to the raiser, who uncharacteristically checks! What is going on? Has he suddenly become timid? Did he miss the flop completely and just does not to waste a bet? Well, no. If he missed the flop, he would bet just in case the others missed as well and they both fold. Instead, he has hit so much of the flop that he feels a need to check and either hope the others catch a second-best hand, or hope they bet into him so he can raise them on the turn for additional large bets. Remarkably, this ploy works a huge number of times, which may be why people keep doing it. (Of course, some players do check occasionally when they miss – I am one – but such players are rare. Those that do check do so for balance, which is covered in detail in Chapter 9.)

Example 1

You limp in late with a hand like 9♠-8♠. The flop comes Q♣-8♦-8♥, there is a bet and call to you, you raise (good play!), and they call. Now the turn is a Q. They check to the raiser (you) and you bet. One of the players calls. Gee, what does he have? Does he have a pair like 9-9, and is calling in the hope that you were raising with nothing? Doe he have an ace, and is calling hoping to get a split pot if you have an ace too, so you both have two pair with the same kicker? Well, no. Almost certainly he has a queen or an eight, and is sitting with a full house. With a queen, he is afraid to check-raise the turn as he does not want to drive you out. When the river comes, he will either bet right out, or check again, hoping to get a check-raise in on the river. Which one depends on how he thinks, and how savvy he thinks you are.

Example 2

Finally, a subtle example. You are in the big blind with J♥-6♦ and get a free play in a six-way pot. The small blind is an expert player. The flop comes 8♥-8♦-2♣, and everyone checks. The turn is the A♣ and everyone checks again. Now the river is the J♠ (giving you jacks and eights with an ace). The pro bets from the small blind. Should you call, raise, or fold? Most players will call here, figuring the pro has a jack, and they will be splitting the pot, but in reality you should fold, as the pro cannot hold a jack. First, there is no point betting a jack (for a thinking player), since nobody will call with anything less at this point, and there are still five players to act. Second, there is no reason to bluff into five players, as there is a decent chance that one of them does hold a jack. So what does the pro have? Possibly an eight, but most likely an ace. Why not bet the ace on the turn? There is little danger in giving a free card if the pro is ahead, and his kicker might not be good. There is also a chance that someone slowplayed an eight on the flop, and the pro does not want to have to decide how to proceed if raised (or waste a bet if it goes bet-raise-reraise). But the river presents an excellent chance to pick up a bet from a player with a jack who might not see the trap.

5. Winning without the best hand

Everyone wins or loses with their aces, kings, queens, and A-K suited. Many times, however, no premium hands are dealt. In these circumstances, the pot does not always go to the player who started with the best hand, or even the one who makes the best hand. The pot sometimes goes to the player who convinces the others that he has the best hand, and does it in such a way that the others fold before the showdown.

Successful bluffing is easiest against players who can also read cards. You paint a picture of a holding you might have that they can clearly see they cannot beat, and they fold. You do not need a hand as much as you need a fine imagination and an ability to look at things from your opponent's perspective. You read from your opponents' actions how likely they are to be strong or weak. You determine from the texture of the flop what sort of hand they might be afraid of. You look at whether your previous actions would have been consistent with your having such a hand. Then you bet/raise to represent it, they believe you, and you take down the pot. Simple, huh?

Of course, it is anything but simple, but it is an acquired skill, and it is something top professionals do daily to win pots to which they are not entitled. Even people who make these plays, however, do it sparingly.

TIP: If you can win one or two pots per night that you are not entitled to, that alone makes a decent hourly rate. Trying too hard or too often destroys your image and makes it impossible to steal much of anything.

6. Inducing calls and bluffs

Making 1 BB per hour requires winning an occasional bet that another player might not realize is available or know how to get. During the play of the hand, pros are always thinking about how to extract the maximum bets from any favorable situation that might arise. When holding what is likely the best hand, they do not just think "bet, bet, bet," but, "how can I play this hand to get the most out of it?" Frequently, this requires playing the hand more slowly, or even with more risk of losing, just to get one extra bet.

For example, in a heads-up situation, a pro has two pair on the turn. After his opponent checks, he feels there is a good likelihood that the opponent will now fold. So instead of betting and winning the pot, he checks. This play may embolden the opponent to bluff the river. Or it may cause enough doubt in the opponent that after a blank falls, and the opponent checks, the pro now bets, and the opponent may make a curiosity call. Either way, the pro makes a bet that a more straightforward player might not get. Of course, the board must be such that the opponent is highly unlikely to be able to use the free card to win the pot.

The smaller the pot, the more necessary it is for you to try to win extra bets. With a large pot, there is less reason to take any risk of losing, and the odds for your opponent to try to beat you may induce him to call your bets anyway.

Chapter 23 – River Play, discusses ways to induce bluffs on that street.

7. Playing the players

Bad players provide most of the income that pros make. Tight pros simply wait until they have a good hand, then play it and hope the bad players are in with their bad hands to add extra money to the pot. However, top pros will alter their hand selection criteria and playing style substantially to allow themselves to be in pots with the bad players.

Most people are familiar with isolation plays, in which a player raises or three-bets another player to eliminate others and get into a head up pot. We have discussed making Illusion of Action plays when weak (or predictable) players are involved. Some pros extend this concept to playing substandard hands if a weak player is involved. Rarer, but still the focus of some top pros, is to forgo a raise (or, more often, a reraise) and simply call if the weak player is behind them and the pro feels the raise might eliminate the poor player. This happens when the weak player in the blind will always stay for one more bet, but not always two.

Example

A tough, aggressive player raises from middle position, and you have A♠-Q♠ on the button. Normally you would three-bet here, as you have good chance of having the best hand and can create dead money from the blinds. But suppose the big blind is a terrible player who always "defends" his blind for one more bet. Now a flat call will get him involved in the hand, and he is a much better source of money than the raiser. Also, the addition of a third player will make the raiser play more honestly and thus predictably than if you and he were heads-up. In this specific situation, calling the raise will be more profitable in the long run than three-betting, even though the big blind player will now win some pots. He will also contribute that much more to the ones you and the raiser will win.

Of course, after the flop, play in such a way as to exploit the specific weakness (calling too much, being too timid, bluffing too often) of the bad player. Playing in this manner will add significantly to your volatility, but the long-range profit from simply being in pots with losing players will eventually create profits.

Conclusion

These strategic methods, plus numerous intangibles (heart, focus, discipline, humor, work ethic, many others), are what separates the players who make a living from the game from those good players who cannot quite figure out why they can't beat the tougher games. These skills do not come easy, but with work and study, you can recognize and eventually make these plays (and the money that goes with them).

Chapter Nine

Balance

Frequently, students ask me what they should look for at the table. Which opponent should they focus on? Should they look for tells or tendencies? How can they remember all of the stuff they are trying to observe?

As a general rule, they should pay attention to the loose players first, and look for tendencies before looking for tells. If you can isolate the tendencies of your opponents, you can read their hands much more easily and play more effectively against them.

However, while you are studying your opponents, some of them are busy studying you. They observe and analyze your play, your style and your specific plays. As a result, you have yet another player to keep close tabs on at the table: yourself!

In fact, almost all top players watch and review their own play with as much energy as they spend on their opponents. What they are striving for is *balance*, that happy state in which their opponents feel unsure of their reads and must guess what to do rather than respond with confidence. In other words, when a player achieves balance in his game, the opponents are off-balance and uncomfortable.

When you make *Illusion of Action* plays, you create balance between your big hands and some others so you can gain action on your powerhouses. But even if you never make that type play, there are many opportunities to create balance by watching your own tendencies and sometimes playing against them.

You would think monitoring your own game would be a lot easier than trying to decipher your opponents' patterns. But for some reason, many players who watch their opponents like a hawk play their own cards almost routinely, making the same plays in the same situations over and over.

In this chapter, we will discuss:

- ♠ What is balance?
- ♠ When is balance important?
- ♠ How do you develop balance?

What is balance?

Most of the time, we play poker straightforwardly. If we have nothing, we fold; if we like our hand, we bet and raise. To keep our play from becoming easily readable, we must occasionally make a different play with the same hand.

For example, you bet the flop and got called. You missed your hand, so you correctly decide to check and fold the turn. So far, so good. But your opponent becomes happily conditioned to the fact that, when you check the turn, he will bet and you will fold. To keep him out of this comfort level, you must sometimes check the turn when you have a real hand, planning to either check-raise the turn or allow your opponent to continue a bluff on the river. When he discovers you are balancing your game by checking good hands as well as bad ones, he will be far less comfortable betting when you check.

Keeping your opponent guessing (off-balance) causes him to make errors, and we all know your opponent's errors result in your profits.

When is balance important?

Overall, balance is the most important aspect in playing in and beating tough games. You want your opponents to feel uncomfortable responding to your bets and raises and even to your checks. Let's look at an example.

Example

Assume you are heads-up and out of position when you get to the end. You have called to the river with a straight draw, but there was also a flush draw on the flop. You decide that if a flush card hits, you will bet out, hoping to represent the flush and get your opponent to fold. That plan sounds good to me.

But what if you are the type of player who, when he makes a flush on the river, always checks hoping to get in a check-raise? Your attempt to represent a flush by betting out will lack credibility to any opponent who has been carefully studying your play. He will simply call. Likewise, if you would have check-raised the flop with a flush draw, your representation now will have no credibility at all and will just be a waste of money.

In this example, we see when you need to really worry about balance:

1. The more aware your opponents are, the more you need to play a balanced game. Some opponents at every table are pretty oblivious, but many are not. The more observant your opponents are, the tougher your game is. These opponents are looking for patterns and willing to act on what they observe.
2. The longer you play with a particular opponent, the more important balance becomes.
3. The fewer opponents you have, the more important balance becomes. In heads-up play, creating balance in your game is vital, and it must always be one of your foremost considerations.

If you play online, your opponents have a huge variety of tools available to help them track your tendencies, summarize them, and make them available at a moment's notice. In addition to the copious notes many of them take, these tools let them easily review every hand you have shown down while they were playing (or sometimes even watching). Even if you think you see a lot of opponents and there is little point in trying to keep up with them all, I assure you that many of them are keeping up with you.

How do you develop balance?

By watching yourself play, you can get a very clear idea of what your trends are. Do you lead on the flop with one pair and always check-raise with two pair? Or do you always lead with two pair hoping to get three bets? Do you raise the flop when you want a free card, but call on the flop with a big hand and wait to raise the turn when the bets double? Do you raise the turn with big draws but wait for the river to raise with huge hands?

Any time you find yourself frequently making predictable plays like these, make a mental note to play against these tendencies in the future. Here are some areas to look for when assessing your game for balance.

Pre-flop

Most players think this is the key area for "varying your play". Personally, I believe that it is far less important than play on the other streets, but there are aspects of pre-flop play that require assessment for balance:

♠ If someone open-raises and you three-bet, do you always have a big pair? Do you always have a pair?

♠ If you cap the betting, do you always have aces or kings?

♠ If you raise out of the blinds, do you always have aces or kings?

On the flop

Many players play very predictably here. Some areas to examine:

♠ If you have a flush draw, do you always bet out? Or do you never bet out?

♠ If you raised pre-flop, will you always bet the flop?

♠ If everyone checks to you on the button, do you always bet?

On the turn

Here are a few areas to think about:

- ♠ If you raise, do you always have a big hand?
- ♠ Likewise, if you bet the flop and check-raise on the turn, do you always have a monster?
- ♠ If you bet and get raised, do you always call?

On the river

- ♠ If you made a draw, do you always bet (or always try for a check-raise)?
- ♠ If you raise, do you always have the near nuts?
- ♠ If you raised the turn, do you always bet?

Notice that I used the word "always" in every example. The message is, if you always play a certain way under a specific circumstance, your game lacks balance. You must make an occasional counter-play so your opponents can't take advantage of your predictability in any area.

Conclusion

The easiest and most profitable opponents to play against are predictable ones. We spend most of our energy trying to find specific areas of predictability in our opponents' games. When we do find them, we exploit them to the limit.

Most people spend a lot less time looking for those areas in their own games. They play the way they play because they feel it is correct and comfortable, while examining the games of others.

The easiest game to examine should be your own. After all, you even know your hole cards every hand. If you look, you will find yourself falling into very repeatable and possibly exploitable patterns. When you find these, think about ways to break the patterns without making completely foolish plays. The more plays you can find that add balance to your game, the tougher opponent you will be.

Part Two: Stages

Pre-flop

Chapter Ten

Pre-flop Hand Values

Starting hand charts are generally an author's shortcut to telling you which hands you will make money on, and under what circumstances, but they don't do a good job of explaining how you can make independent decisions. Unlike blackjack, playing to a hand chart without thinking can get you into a lot of trouble.

A hand chart is a way to get you started playing poker, but the decisions you make must consider why the hand chart was formulated and what it means. Because you have found a chart that says that A-10 is approximately equal to 8-6 suited doesn't mean that A-10 and 8-6 suited are interchangeable, and that you can play both similarly. In fact, they play differently depending on the circumstances, which chart creators try to explain in the text. Despite this, too many players seem to follow charts without thinking about or understanding the context.

Let me try a different approach. Let's divide the world of playable hands into three categories:

- ♠ Power hands (P)
- ♠ Volume hands (V)
- ♠ Hybrid hands (H)

Hybrid hands combine power and volume qualities.

Power hands

Power hands contain high cards. If you hold a power hand, you may be able to win unimproved, but you generally hope to make one pair and hope it holds up. For example, if you have A-Q, you are trying to either

1. Win because your hand is better than the other hands, or
2. Make a pair that you hope is best with the best kicker.

Certainly you can make straights and full houses with these cards, but your primary goal is to make a pair and have it stand up. For example, if you have A-J you would much rather play heads-up than against seven opponents. With A-J you are still trying to make one pair. Against seven players, the combined chances that you will flop a pair, and that it will hold up to win are too small to even get involved. *Power hands play best in short-handed pots.*

Volume hands

Volume hands are suited connectors, suited one-gappers, suited aces, and small pairs. A hand like 9-8 suited or 3-3 doesn't play well heads-up. Let's see why.

You don't want to take 9-8 suited against one opponent who has a playable hand because it is very hard to win. If he has A-Q, and you don't improve, you lose. If you both improve to one pair, you lose. If you flop a draw heads-up, you will not get the right price to make your draw.

Limit players who watch no-limit tournaments on TV frequently fall in love with small pairs because announcers constantly reinforce the notion that small pairs are favorites against overcards like A-K. They are if there is no further betting, but very tough to play when your opponent may have a wide variety of hands, and you have just a small pair. With a flop of J♦-9♠-7♠, how do you feel about your 3♥-3♣?

If your opponent has A-K, great. If he has any pair higher then yours, a jack, nine, or seven, you are drawing thin. If he has 10-8 you are drawing nearly dead. Even if you are ahead and an eight hits, can you call a bet? You still beat A-K, K-Q, and A-Q, but lose to almost any other hand he can have. If all of the money is in the middle and the hands are face up, you can see where you stand, but playing your tiny pair with three more rounds of betting to play through will be quite difficult.

On the other hand, if you take 9-8 suited up against seven players, you won't make a winning hand all that often, but, when you do make one, it will usually be a straight or a flush. A straight or a flush is going to win a lot of money. What does that have to do with EV?

Let's say you play 9-8 suited against my A-Q heads-up. You'll still make the same number of straights and flushes as if you went against a seven-handed field. The trouble is that there will only be two people betting into the pot, and the number of straights and flushes you make won't compensate for the number you miss, because the pots are going to be small. With seven players, when you flop a straight or flush draw, you'll get the right pot odds to draw for it. *Volume hands play best in multiway pots.*

Hybrid hands

Hybrid hands play well in both short-handed and multiway pots. There are two varieties of hybrid hands:

1. Big suited cards
2. Big pairs

1. Big suited cards

Big suited cards (like A-J suited and A-K suited) have power value in short-handed pots because they are comprised of high cards, and they have volume value because they can make flushes. If they are also connected, like K-Q suited, straight chances come more into play as well.

If you have A♣-K♦, if you don't flop an ace or a king, you can't be all that happy. But if you have A♥-K♥, you are happy if you flop an ace, a king, or a couple of hearts. If you flop a couple of hearts, you'd still rather have a bunch of people in, because when you make your hand, you want to play for a nice-sized pot.

2. Big pairs

Big pairs are A-A through 10-10. These hands can frequently win short-handed pots unimproved, making them good power hands. They can also win in multiway situations because they can make sets, or even win a rare pot when no one else improves and the one pair stands up. To be sure, A-A is a far better hand than 10-10, but they can be considered roughly in the same category.

Summary

If you understand which type of hand you hold, you are better prepared to make the correct play for the situation in which you find yourself. This is one reason why pre-flop position is so important. If you are under the gun with 9-8 suited, you can't say to yourself, "I'll just limp in and maybe this will be a volume pot," because maybe it won't be. If maybe it will and maybe it won't, then you are gambling, and you don't want to gamble any more than you have to.

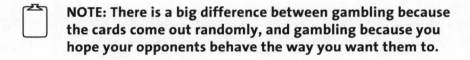 **NOTE: There is a big difference between gambling because the cards come out randomly, and gambling because you hope your opponents behave the way you want them to.**

You want to put yourself in situations that you know are +EV. The only hands you can play up front are the top power hands and hybrid hands, because it doesn't much matter how many opponents there are – the hands will still play decently. Raise to try to thin the field, and to make sure that players who wish to enter with inferior hands pay a higher entry fee.

Play volume hands only when you are confident you will get at least four opponents and preferably more. If there is a raise and two callers to you in the cutoff, your call with a volume hand depends on what you think of the remaining players. If at least one of them tends to call liberally, go ahead and call. If they all fold, the dead money from the blinds folding compensates somewhat for the lack of the fourth player.

The number of opponents is more important than the number of bets you need to pay to play volume hands. With six or more, you can pay a cap to play hands like small pairs and suited aces.

Chapter Eleven

Pre-flop Hand Selection

This chapter presents an analysis of playable hands, and discusses briefly how to evaluate them pre-flop. Because I could spend a lot of time on each hand, the descriptions will be brief and just highlight the most important features. Each hand will also have a letter designating its primary attribute as a power (P), volume (V), or hybrid (H) hand.

My recommendations are somewhat tighter than you will find in other books. I recommend that you play tighter with middle pairs, A-10, most suited kings, and low suited connectors because I see many players struggling with these hands out of position.

I also see knowledgeable players exhibit looser standards than "the books" say. They do it because:

- ♠ They overestimate their ability.
- ♠ They underestimate their opponents.
- ♠ They get bored.
- ♠ They overvalue marginal hands because they have been lucky with them and think the hands are winners. This is the trap of random reinforcement.
- ♠ They have reasonable overall results and don't believe that their results could be better if they stopped playing certain hands.

If I tell you to play pairs down to 10-10 under the gun (which I do) and you play 9-9, nothing terrible will happen. I think it is a lifetime loser, but not by much.

Every player needs a bedrock foundation game to play that will win in the long run. This chapter provides that. Use it when you are unsure of the game, not playing your best, or if the game you are in rewards straightforward poker, as many do.

You can play beyond this structure to take advantage of situational opportunities, or to make an occasional *Illusion of Action* play as the game demands. If you are an experienced player, this situational play approach will provide better results and fewer difficult decisions than an overall looser approach. However, to deviate from this method, you need to be able to articulate *why* you are doing it (at least to yourself). "I have not played a hand in an hour," is not a good reason. "This is a tight, observant table, and I am fairly sure my opponents will all fold if I raise here unless they hold premium hands, because they have all noticed and commented that I have not played a hand in an hour," is a good reason.

Understand the situation and reasons for playing more hands or playing them differently. Even the hands I tell you "never" to play may have exceptions. For example, if you are on the button with many terrible players in the game, and they all limp, go ahead and call with 4-3 suited. In the long run, it may be profitable, and you may win a great deal if you flop a miracle. It also has *Illusion of Action* value.

In the discussion that follows, hands are discussed with respect to their merit in normal play. There are two significant non-standard situations: blind steals, and play from the blinds. Chapter 12 discusses blind steals, and Chapter 13 covers blind play. Neither of these is covered in this chapter. Also, *Illusion of Action* plays are primarily position-, image-, and opponent-related rather than hand-related. You need to keep the value of your hand in mind, but for purely situational plays, it is not of primary importance. When assessing a hand, keep in mind that the important questions to ask pre-flop are:

- ♠ What sort of hand are you hoping to make?
- ♠ What circumstances do you need for your cards to be profitable?
- ♠ How likely is it those circumstances exist?

In limit hold'em, pocket pairs and big cards represent almost all of the hands you should play, and they are the source of most of your profits. In addition, some other hand types are playable in volume pots. We will look at all the hands you should play in that order:

- ♠ Pocket pairs
- ♠ Big cards
- ♠ Other hands

Pocket Pairs

These hands vary from the strongest hand in poker to ones that can be played only in high volume or steal situations. Here is a breakdown:

A-A (H)

Raise. I don't care about game, position, type of opponents, or loss of deception. When you see aces pre-flop in a limit game, raise. Some people advocate open-calling with aces on occasion, planning to use this deception later, either by reraising a pre-flop raiser or by making a big hidden hand later. Many of them are very good players, and this play may work for them (or seem to). But A-A is not just a little better than other starting hands – it is a *lot* better. Because it frequently wins without improvement, failing to raise gives up significant pre-flop equity.

There is one more point about pocket aces. They do not always win. Yes, I realize you knew that, but some people play as if this fact comes as a complete shock. They will cling to the aces until the showdown in spite of all the evidence that they cannot win this particular pot. Then they show everyone their hand, hoping to get the sympathy they think they deserve. Do not fall into this trap. If you feel your hand is no good, even if it is A-A, lay it down – *face down*. Only your mother and spouse care about your bad luck.

K-K (H)

Raise. Again, anytime you see kings pre-flop, raising cannot be a bad idea. You have a huge edge over any hand but aces, and unless you are confident that you are against aces, you should be raising.

I have seen players limp with kings because they want to see if the flop has an ace before they commit their chips to the pot. This play has two drawbacks. First, they encourage players with hands like A-x to enter, so if an ace does hit, they become huge dogs. Second, they allow players with undercards to enter the pot cheaply and attempt to crack their kings. One of the reasons to raise pre-flop with premium hands is to make it expensive for opponents to enter, so they are making a bigger mistake to do so than if you called. Also, it may be the last chance to get extra money in the pot, since your opponents may fold if they do not like the flop.

Q-Q, J-J (H)

These are very good hands, of course, and normally worth a raise or reraise. The raise enlarges the pot but, more importantly, may eliminate players with an overcard who might call one small pre-flop bet, but not two or three. With these hands you are hoping to have an overpair to the flop, and collect money from folks who will call you down with a smaller pair (usually hoping you are overplaying A-K or A-Q). The hybrid nature of the hands comes from the fact that they can still flop sets and take down large pots even in big fields.

A major exception is Q-Q and J-J in the big blind. Do not raise from this spot against more than two opponents. You can no longer eliminate players by raising. When overcard(s) flop (one third of the time for Q-Q, over half the time for J-J), you want to be able to fold quickly and cheaply if there is much action, since you are generally not getting the right price to continue.

More importantly, if you flop an overpair, you want to raise someone to eliminate players with overcards. If you raise pre-flop, you will generally bet on the flop, and opponents will often call with overcards given the large pot you have built. If you just check pre-flop from the big blind in a multiway pot, someone with a pair or draw might bet, allowing you to raise if it is the small blind, or check-raise. This raise will either eliminate the players with overcards or force them to pay a higher price, increasing your EV.

Failure to raise with these hands sacrifices current equity (raising pre-flop with the best hand) to gain equity later through strategic play combined with your opponents' misreads as they will not put you on a hand this strong. Controlling pot size, eliminating opponents, folding cheaply to dangerous flops, and gaining action from second-best hands more than makes up for the loss of pre-flop raising equity.

The discussion above is also true for the small blind, except when you feel you can eliminate the big blind by raising. If you can't, just call and wait to make a play later, if possible.

Another note about Q-Q and J-J is that you can lay these hands down before the flop. I have never folded A-A or K-K pre-flop in a limit cash game, but I have occasionally folded Q-Q or J-J.

Example

Here is a Q-Q fold: An extremely tight professional raised from under the gun in a $20-$40 game. Everyone folded to another extremely tight professional who reraised from the small blind. Goodbye, pocket queens in the big blind. I was 100 percent certain I was against at least one overpair, which made my queens a huge underdog.

10-10 (H)

This is the worst pocket pair you should play in early position. You will see an overcard flop (and no set for you) almost 60 percent of the time, and you will not know how to play this hand out of position. Open-raise to eliminate players and attempt to play against one or two at most. In very tough games with players three-betting liberally, you may not want to play this hand at all in early position.

Once you get to middle position, it is an excellent hand to open-raise and to reraise loose raisers. If a tight player open-raises early, fold 10-10 behind him.

9-9, 8-8 (H)

Fold these hands in early position; open-raise in middle position. Fold to a pre-flop raise unless the raiser is a very poor player, in which case three-bet.

9-9 and 8-8 play well against one or two opponents, and lose a lot of value against three or four opponents, and then play well again as a volume hand against five or more. Your objective is to limit the field if possible and expand the field otherwise. If you may be against three or four players, fold the hand rather than gamble on getting into a volume situation.

In late position raise a single limper, especially if there is a decent chance to create a heads-up or three-way pot.

Small Pairs (7-7 – 2-2) (V)

Yes, I know 7-7 is better than 2-2, but in most multiway pots they play similarly. You do not to expect to flop an overpair, so you hope to flop a set. You will flop a set or better around one time in eight, and you need a volume pot to invest in the chance that you will hit. You will make more money most of the time you do make a set, as at least some of the opponents will continue to play with pair hands, drawing nearly dead, because they will be seduced by the size of the pot.

These hands are very positional. You want to play against five or more opponents. You do not want to put in three bets to see a flop four-handed. Therefore, you should play these hands only in the last three positions where you can get a good feel for how many bets you will need to put in, and how many opponents there will be.

In tight games, where multiway pots are infrequent, resist the temptation to raise with these cards from middle position in an attempt to win the blinds or get heads-up. Your success rate will likely not be enough to justify expending money on these mediocre hands.

In tight games, players fall in love with the idea of three-betting a single player who has raised. This seems attractive, as it will get you heads-up with the initiative against a player who may well have only big cards. You will have some success if you do this, but overall I believe it to be a losing play unless you are making an *Illusion of Action* variant. First, you may not isolate the player, in which case your hand will be difficult to play. Second, he may have, make, or represent a pocket or flopped pair. Third, you may be reraised and elect to call to the river to see if he has a pair or A-K.

As an *Illusion of Action* play, raise a loose raiser, or a single raiser in late position, when you are the cutoff or the button. He is more likely to be stealing then, and you want to eliminate the blinds and go heads-up with him. Otherwise, fold and wait for more favorable circumstances.

It is hard to lay down pairs, I know. But it is one of the first signs of a truly maturing player.

Big Cards

This section discusses hands containing two cards with letters in the corners (A, K, Q, and J). In general, you are trying to make top pair with a good kicker and have it hold up. This means big cards play best against few opponents. In large multiway pots, unsuited big cards lose a lot of their value; one pair will typically not be enough to win. It will hold up sometimes, but you must also be prepared to get off the hand if you are challenged.

Pre-flop, your main goal is to reduce the field if possible and to keep the pot small if you can't. Because these goals conflict, you will need to judge whether your raise will eliminate people. If players in your game tend to ignore raises, make them more sparingly.

Suited big cards play better against a large field because a flopped flush draw will allow you to see the turn when you have not flopped a pair or better. In addition, when you do make a flush in a volume pot and win, your profit will be large. Therefore, you can play suited big cards strongly pre-flop even with a larger field.

If you play in loose games, you should avoid all unsuited big card hands except A-K and A-Q. One of the reasons players have such a hard time in these games is that they play hands like K-J, which look nice but play poorly six-handed or higher. These hands are drawing to make marginal one-pair hands which are vulnerable to overcards, better kickers, and the fact that in large fields, one pair does not hold up often.

A-K (P)

These premium cards play well against a small field. Raise all the time except when there are four or more limpers. With several players already in, do not raise out of the blinds.

Your objective in raising with A-K offsuit is to thin the field. Once the field is already large, you are better off waiting for the flop to play strategically, raising if you hit your hand and generally folding (depending on pot size and flop texture) if no help appears. Again, as in the case of Q-Q and J-J in the blinds discussed earlier, you are sacrificing current equity for improved strategic opportunities by not raising pre-flop in large fields.

A-Ks (H)

Unlike A-K offsuit, you can raise with this hand in any position and against any number of players. You still need to play it carefully post-flop.

A-Q (P)

This is a much tougher hand to play. Enter raising following the rules for A-K. However, in very tough games, fold this hand in early position (and find a better game). Also, be careful calling raises with it. If a tight player raises in early position in front of you, fold. If a loose player raises in front of you, three-bet.

A-Qs (H)

You can play it like A-K suited almost all of the time. Do not raise from the blinds as much, as it is harder to win unimproved and a king can hit the board, giving you only one overcard. It is OK to call an early raise from a tight player if you believe you can induce multiway action, but in general, you should raise or fold depending on how much control you believe you have over the raiser.

A-J (P)

Fold this hand in early position. In middle or late position treat it like A-Q.

A-Js (H)

Play this hand up front in all but the toughest games (open-raising, of course). Do not call early raises.

K-Q (P)

While this hand does not have an ace, it still has a reasonable chance to make top pair with a winning kicker. However, do not play in a raised pot unless you are the raiser, or three-betting a loose raiser in late position. Do not play this hand in early position. It's hard to play on all streets out of position because you can easily be dominated.

K-Qs (H)

I like large suited connectors and do not mind playing this hand in multiway pots for several bets. Raise in early position unless your game is tough, in which case fold until early-middle position, then raise. If you narrow the field, you can use the power aspects of the hand, and if you happen to attract players, you can use its valuable volume potential. Raise several limpers, as you do not mind large pots.

K-J (P)

While it looks pretty with those pictures staring back at you, K-J is really the beginning of the mediocre hands that get people in trouble. Play only in late position if you can get in cheaply. Don't call raises with this hand. Open-raise in the power position (button minus 2) or later.

K-Js (H)

Not much better than K-J, this hand does not play as well as K-Q suited by any means. If you flop a king, you have the third best kicker and cannot be aggressive. If you flop a jack, you are vulnerable to two overcards instead of one. More flops offer straight potential to connectors than to one-gappers. Again, do not play this hand early, and do not raise with it late unless you are the first one in. Do not call raises unless, of course, you have already put in one bet.

Q-J (P)

This hand has been called "Hawaii" because with all of the money you save by not playing it, you can afford a trip to that island paradise. You can play it late for one bet, but that's about it. Open-raise from the power position and later.

Q-Js (H)

This is a much better hand than Q-J offsuit. It does not work well with few opponents, however, so make sure you are getting multiway action or open-raise in late position to get heads-up and use the power value of this hand.

Other Hands

You can play several other hands under specific circumstances, but you may be seduced by boredom, optimism, or lack of knowledge into playing inappropriately. These hands include:

- ♠ Ace-x
- ♠ Ace-x suited
- ♠ King-x suited or not
- ♠ Connectors
- ♠ Suited connectors
- ♠ One-gap hands
- ♠ Suited one-gap hands
- ♠ Bigger gaps

With the exception of A-x, you hope to flop draws with these hands. That means they almost always need a large field and a small entry price (one bet). If both conditions are met, play these hands. If there is more than one bet to you, you need a huge field (five or more opponents) to play.

Ace-x (P)

Play A-10 in late position against one or two limpers, raising if you think you can eliminate the other players. Against more players you should fold it. Do not call raises with A-10, but if you are in late position against a late position raise, three-bet.

Raise with A-9 in position against one limper. Other hands are used for blind steals only (see Chapter 12).

In all other circumstances fold these hands without a thought. More money has probably been lost playing A-rag than any other hand because so many people play it when they shouldn't. It usually makes only top-pair-bad-kicker or bad-pair-top-kicker. If there is any action, either one of these is a loser.

Ace-x suited (V)

This hand is considerably better because of the nut-flush possibilities. You are trying to flop a flush draw and make it. You might win with the ace, of course, but that is not the objective. You need either to get in cheaply or have many opponents. In tight games, play it in middle or late position, and only against three or more limpers. Otherwise, follow the guidelines for A-x.

K-x suited or not

Forget it. I see lots of people playing K-x suited, and they are almost always wrong. None of the hands you are trying to make are particularly good (non-nut flush, pair of kings with a bad kicker). In particular, lots of players seem to think K-10 is a good hand in some spots. It isn't, except for blind steals and *Illusion of Action* plays.

Connectors (V)

Connectors are two cards together, like 9-8 or 5-4. We covered A-K, K-Q, and Q-J above, so here we are looking at J-10 down to 3-2. Let's start from the bottom to make this quick. Never play 6-5, 5-4, 4-3, and 3-2. Play 7-6 and 8-7 on the button for one bet with at least three limpers. That leaves us with J-10 and 10-9. I am partial to J-10 because it makes a maximum number of straights, and every straight it makes is the nuts. It also has some chance to make top pair, although that is not its true value.

Both J-10 and 10-9 need a lot of company. You are aiming to flop a straight draw and want good pot odds to make it and to be paid off if you do. In loose games you can play these hands in middle or late position for one bet. In tight games, they are rarely playable.

Suited connectors (V)

Again, I am talking here about suited, connected cards from J-10 through 3-2. Having your connectors in the same suit adds a lot of value to your pre-flop hand, as there are more good flops. Nevertheless, they are still not premium hands and you need good circumstances to play them.

Again from the bottom, never play 3-2, 4-3, or 5-4 suited. I know they are fun to play and a lot of laughs when you win with them, but you are playing for money, not laughs. (If you *are* playing for laughs, 3-2 suited is a great hand to raise with. On the rare occasion that you win with it, you can turn it over and get a day's worth of chuckles!) Play 6-5, 7-6, and 8-7 suited in middle or late position for one bet as long as two or more players are already in. Play J-10 suited and 10-9 suited in middle or late position in a loose-passive game. In an aggressive game, these hands lose value in middle position, as raises and small fields become too likely. Play them only in late position for one bet. In a tight game, you can still play J-10 suited for one bet in middle or late position if there are two or more players.

One-gap hands

One-gap hands are connectors with a one-card hole in the middle. We covered A-Q and K-J before. Now we can look at Q-10 through 4-2. It is harder to flop a straight draw with one-gap hands than it is with connectors[6], and they are therefore less valuable. Since we have seen that connectors have little value, imagine what we should think of one-gappers.

Never play 4-2, 5-3, 6-4, 7-5, and 8-6. If the game is loose, and the players are poor, you can play 9-7 and 10-8 on the button for one bet if three or more players are already in. Otherwise, fold. With three or more players and no raise, play J-9 or Q-10 in the last two positions for one bet.

Suited one-gap hands

You can play suited one-gappers in position earlier than their offsuit counterparts. Never play 6-4, 5-3, or 4-2 suited. Play 8-6 suited and 7-5 suited on the button for one bet with limpers. On the high end, play Q-10 suited and J-9 suited in middle position in a loose game with a couple of players already in. All these hands still play for one (initial) bet only. Never call a raise cold with any suited one-gap hand below A-Qs.

Bigger gaps

We have already considered A-J. K-10 is the next largest two-gap hand, and it really is not playable. Many players enter pots with it, or even call raises, but you really do not want to have this hand in a multiway pot.

---

[6] Middle connectors can flop three open-ended straight draws and six gutshots. Middle one-gappers can flop two open-ended straight draws and five gutshots.

Any two-gap hand below that is even worse, as are three-gap hands. In late position for a single bet you can play K-10 suited and Q-9 suited, but be very careful. The only two straights you can make with Q-9, for example, are with boards containing J-10-8 or K-J-10. In the latter case, A-Q is the nuts and could easily be out against you. K-10 suited or not and Q-9 suited are decent blind steal hands from the cutoff or button.

With J-8 or below, suited or not, you are better off mucking and waiting for a better opportunity.

Summary

This style makes you play very tight up front, and fairly tight in later positions. In tight games, you cannot play many hands at all, and in aggressive games, you can play still fewer. If you find yourself putting in two bets on mediocre hands, tighten up your play.

Situationally, you can vary from this in any direction (tighter, looser, more aggressive, even more passive) when you understand the issues and make thoughtful plays. Poker is a game that rewards the player with patience who can wait for premium hands or good value with position, then exploit the edge they give him. Strive to be that player, and you will gain those rewards.

Chapter Twelve

Stealing the Blinds

If everyone folds to you in late position, you may want to raise to try to win the blinds. Putting the players to your left in the blinds under constant pressure to either fold or play marginal hands out of position is one of the keys to making extra money.

Before making this play, consider these factors:

- Your position.
- The opponents' tendencies.
- Your image.

Your position

You can make this raise from the button, the cutoff, or the position to the right of the cutoff, which has been called various names (I term it the "power position"). Let's look at each position.

The button

This is the most obvious steal position, but that should not stop you from open-raising with a variety of hands. As in most hold'em situations, your opponents' tendencies to call and the quality of their post-flop play will influence your decision. We will look at these in the next section. In general, you still want to have high cards, so any two cards eight or higher will do fine. Also, raise with all pairs, all suited aces, offsuit aces down to A-6, and suited connectors down to 7-6 suited.

Notice that this recommended set of hands excludes most hands with twos through fives, except for suited aces. Small cards present difficult play problems, and eliminating small cards from your repertoire will avoid tiny underpair problems that often make for difficult stay-or-fold decisions. There is a popular notion that A-2 through A-5 play better than A-6 because they can make some straights. They also make small pairs and smaller kickers far more often than they make straights. Ace-rag does represent a chance to open up your game if necessary, but avoid these hands most of the time.

The cutoff

You have to worry about the button as well as the blinds, so you need a slightly better hand. Open-raise with all hands with two cards nine or higher, all pairs, suited aces down to A-6, and offsuit aces down to A-8.

The power position

I draw a bright line between the positions two off the button and three off the button. There are still four players to act behind you, but raises here have a credibility factor that raises in the cutoff and button do not have. You are risking more when you make the raise, but you are also more likely to get respect for your hand quality. Thus, your chances to win the blinds uncontested go up, and your chances to win after the flop increase as well. Hands that are routine folds in any earlier position become raising hands in the power position. These include any two Broadway cards, suited aces to A-7, A-9 offsuit, K-9 suited, and pairs down to 6-6.

Your opponents' tendencies

Because you must always play a situational game, continuously adapt your opponents' stealing strategies. In particular, study the tendencies of:

- ♠ The blinds.
- ♠ Players with position on you.

The Blinds

If they are unusually tight and rarely call raises, increase your raising frequency. Sometimes, a player will flash you an ace or king as he lays down his big blind to your steal raise. He is doing this to show you how well he (thinks he) plays. He does not want to get into kicker trouble out of position. Since you now know he is severely limiting the hands he will call with, at least against you, raise his blind more liberally.

Many opponents call raises from the blinds far too liberally, some even going so far as to never lay down a hand. If both blinds play like this, you can never win uncontested and must alter your strategy. This situation is the inverse of the too-tight blinds, and you therefore must tighten up your raising standards, particularly on the button.

Raises from the power position and cutoff serve two potential purposes:

- ♠ Winning the blinds.
- ♠ Improving your position by getting the late position players to fold.

When you already have the button, and no one else has entered, the primary reasons to raise change. As the button, you raise with your better hands because you likely have a heavily-favored hand and will be playing against random cards. However, when there is no opportunity to get either blind to fold, raising loses some of its importance. Somewhat counter-intuitively, it becomes reasonable to open-limp on the button with some of the weaker hands you would like to play, such as 7-6 suited and small pairs. Also, limping on the button with weak offsuit aces works well, because they are not heavily favored against random hands, and because you may get extra action when an ace comes, as these loose players may automatically assume you would have raised on the button with an ace.

Players with position on you

Of equal importance are the tendencies of the players to act behind you. The better they play and, in particular, the more likely they are to challenge you with reraises, the tighter you have to play. You are making these light raises to gain an advantage, not to try to outplay a tough player who has position and potentially a better hand.

Conversely, if the players between you and the blinds are timid and will almost always fold or at worst call your raises, you can focus more on the tendencies of the blinds, and potentially open up even more when the blinds are tight. Timid players who readily concede their position to raises are plentiful. Recognize them, and be ready to exploit them when you get the right circumstances.

Your image

Aware opponents will eventually react to your raises and play back at you somehow. Of course, sometimes they will actually hold excellent hands. However, other times, they will make plays because your late position raising frequency indicates that you do not have premium hands, and they think they can bet you off your mediocre holdings.

You need to make two adjustments. First, of course, you can play tighter and rehabilitate your image. But you also need to realize that some of the action you are getting from the blinds may be more related to their perception of you than the value of their hands (in other words, you have created the *Illusion of Action*). Call down more liberally when you realize that you have a loose, aggressive image, as you will have induced excess action by your previous play.

When you have, by virtue of not holding any decent hands, developed a tight image, use that perception by making an occasional out-of-line late position raise as a blind steal. Your win frequency against observant, tight opponents will be excellent. Remember, though, that people playing back at you have real hands, because they respect your raises and are still challenging you.

Conclusion

Stealing the blinds is more complex than just raising with any two cards when everyone folds to you. First, you should have raising standards, though you may choose to violate them circumstantially. Second, constantly evaluate your opponents' abilities and their image of you in determining when to execute this play.

You make steal raises to win money, not to show off. If the opponents are tough or your image is weak, make this play only with good hands. If the opponents are weak and your image is strong, you do not need much to win. Be aware of this, and your steals will pressure the opposition, annoy the players to your left, and make profits both from their folds and their excess action borne of frustration.

Chapter Thirteen

Blind Play

If you play in a ten-handed game, you spend 20% of your time in the blinds. Despite this fact, players and authors spend much more time thinking about every other position than they do about blind play. This chapter covers most of the common issues associated with playing the blinds in a full ring game. These include:

- ♠ Universal considerations.
- ♠ Playing after a "steal raise".
- ♠ Playing after a non-steal raise.
- ♠ Playing the small blind with no raise.
- ♠ Playing the big blind with no raise.
- ♠ Blind vs. blind.
- ♠ Playing trash hands out of the blinds.

Universal considerations

(Keep these concepts in mind regardless of the specific situation you face during blind play.)

1. Expectation.
2. Position.
3. Emotionally charged words.
4. Pot odds.

1. Expectation

Over the course of your poker career, you will lose money in the blinds. People hate hearing and believing this, but it's true. No matter how well you play, it is simply a terrible idea to put money into a pot out of position without looking at your hand. No amount of post-flop skill can make up for it. Obviously, like in the rest of poker, some people will lose more than others, but all of us will be net losers in the blind positions.

Therefore, one of your goals is simply to minimize your losses. I am not telling you just to fold without looking, but, if you play the blinds in a way that loses more than you would have by folding without looking, you clearly need to reassess your play.

Since you lose money in the blinds, you would lose more if you elected to straddle. Therefore, always be alert to the possibility that your opponents may straddle and encourage them to do so.

2. Position

You will act first or second on every one of the next three betting rounds. You will have to commit chips before you know what the others will do, or you will have to check and then guess whether they are betting because you have checked, or betting because they have you beat. Otherwise you will be giving up free cards.

I don't want to turn this into a treatise on position, but most players underestimate the importance of position in limit hold'em, even if they give it weight in no-limit. In an activity where many consider one bet per hour a gold standard for expert play, much of that extra bet comes from betting, raising, or folding in position.

Craving action, one student tried hard to argue that he could play all sorts of hands out of the blind when faced with an early position raise. His thesis was that they probably had big cards, and he could take the pot away whenever small cards came. I gave him the following mantra: *"You cannot make money playing a mediocre hand out of position against a good player with a better hand."* It's not catchy, but I recommend you memorize it anyway.

3. Emotionally charged words

One of the most disastrous words in gambling is "defend". This word has connotations of bravery, combat, machismo, and all that good stuff. The opposite of defend is what? Give up? Surrender? Concede? These all sound so wimpy. Real men (and women) defend what they have: their family, their honor, and their possessions.

So what does all of this have to do with blind play? Actually, nothing at all, but that's the word we have come to associate with deciding whether to throw more money in the pot when the blind has been raised. Is someone who raises your blind really "attacking" it? Sometimes, maybe, but usually he is simply trying to charge you more with your unknown hand to continue to play against his superior holding.

Your decision to put more money into a pot should be the same whether you are in the blind or have already made a bet and been raised. Does the value of your hand combined with the price the pot is offering provide a positive expectation? If yes, play; if not, fold. Defending has nothing to do with it.

If you must associate a word with putting more money in when your blind is raised, I suggest you try "chase". "Do I want to chase the money I already put in?" sounds more realistic than, "Do I want to defend my blind?"

Another emotionally charged word that has become associated with blind play is "discount" or "half-price". Wow! A bargain! You only have to put one small bet into the pot to call a raise. Who can resist such a deal? Obviously, all of the above arguments apply. You do not want to invest in damaged goods, even at a discount.

4. Pot odds

Repeatedly, I have seen players toss in money chasing their blind (it does have a ring, yes?) while reciting "pot odds, pot odds." What these folks forget is that there are two pieces to pot odds. One is the price the pot offers you. The other is the actual chance that you will win more than the money you are investing.

Suppose I were to telephone you from a local sports book. "There is a bet on the board of 15-to-1," I tell you. "How much do want to get down?" You would naturally ask what it was you were betting on. If it were the chances for a Pop Warner team to win the Super Bowl this year, you would pass.

But if you see a few bets in the pot, should you toss in an extra bet with 8-3 or Q-6 or 5-2 in the blind regardless because of "pot odds?" Not unless you know that the chances of winning are greater than that price, and frequently they are not.

Pot odds are nice to have, but you must understand both sides of the equation.

Playing after a "steal raise"

Most people are more concerned about reacting to "steal" raises than any other aspect of blind play, judging by the questions students ask. And no wonder. You are sitting in a nice limit poker game in the big blind. Everyone folds to the button, who raises. The small blind folds. You hold something mediocre, say, J-9, or K-5, or 8-6 suited. It feels wimpy just to throw your not terrible hand away, and it feels a bit foolish to call a raise with this cheese. What to do?

The same holds true for the small blind, who not only has to put in more money than the big blind, but also has to worry about the big blind waking up with a hand and about being out of position to two players.

On the other hand, so many players on the button will raise with a wide variety of hands (a few with any hand) that laying down what could easily be the best hand when getting odds to call does not sit well with most players. What to do?

What is a steal raise?

Steal raises are covered more completely in Chapter 12 – Stealing the Blinds.

Briefly, all of the players must have folded to late position player who raises. Many players raise with a variety of hands hoping to get the blinds to fold, or to gain the post-flop initiative and force the blinds to make a hand to continue after the flop.

The Cardinal Rule

Start with what I call the Cardinal Rule for blind play against any raise, but particularly against a steal raise. Here it is:

> *The better the player who raised, the fewer hands you should play.*

Talk about a dangerous rule! When I tell students this rule, they relax right away and start playing too many hands. After all, the guy who raised is never very good, according to the blinds. Please be realistic about this.

You need to understand one more aspect of steal raises here. Some players don't make them. In fact, some players don't even make value raises in late position. They just play tight. Against them, it is sheer folly to play mediocre hands because they raised in late position, since they don't reduce their raising standards. They are never stealing. Thus, we get another rule:

> *The tighter the player who raised, the fewer hands you should play.*

There is one additional quick rule to look at. Most players treat steal raises in the cut-off and raises on the button as the same animal, but they aren't. While some players will raise with almost any two on the button, the same players need *some* values to raise from the cut-off. Even light raisers realize that they are vulnerable to a reraise by the button. So we can include a third rule:

> *Play fewer hands against a steal raiser in the cut-off than from the button.*

Keep these rules in mind as we continue this discussion. I can't repeat them each time we discuss hand selection, but they still must dominate your thoughts and actions.

Play from the small blind

Let's start by looking at the small blind. Which hands should you play, and how should you play them?

The default play is to reraise any hand you are going to play. This is consistent with the fact that the small blind's play follows the criteria set forth for a raise or fold situation defined in Chapter 7.

You may find this painful, as there will be hands you would like to play, but not for at least three bets pre-flop out of position. If you call the steal raise, the big blind gets odds of 5-to-1 to call. If you reraise, the big blind must call two more bets with only six in the pot (3-to-1) and face the possibility of a reraise from the original raiser. Obviously, this cuts down significantly on the hands the big blind will play.

If your reraise gets the big blind to fold, you have created dead money, the big blind will not be able to draw out or flop a miracle, and you will be out of position to only one player rather than two. These are powerful reasons to put in that raise.

In general, play any hand you would open-raise with if you were in late middle position. Make this play with pairs down to 6-6, any two Broadway cards, any suited ace, and offsuit aces down to A-9. If you want to add more hands (perhaps because this is a game in which the button is really pounding your blind round after round), add suited hands like 10-9, K-9, Q-9, and 9-8.

Three-betting with these may get you some strange looks, but they are consistent with the *Illusion of Action*. You can make a technically correct play and still look like a real action junkie to an unsophisticated player. He will not understand how you can three-bet with a hand like Q-9 suited.

Are there times you should not reraise from the small blind? Yes, a few.

- ♠ If the big blind plays terribly, you might not want to raise him out, especially if he will chase incorrectly, call raises with inadequate values, never bluff, and pay off on the river with second-best hand.

- ♠ In live play, if you see the big blind ready to fold before you play, calling and seeing the flop is often a good idea, as it helps convince the steal raiser that you have a big hand when you do three-bet.

- ♠ If the steal raiser is highly aggressive (he will bet the flop and turn and perhaps the river on any two cards), you can call with a few good hands and check-raise on the turn or river in an attempt to win the pot and slow down future steal attempts.

♠ In a tight game, where a steal raiser gets frequent chances to be first in, vary your three-betting and calling so he does not get used to you three-betting with moderate hands. Balancing your play this way requires that you call with some suited hands, as well as some excellent ones,

♠ If the big blind never folds, just call with all but your premium hands.

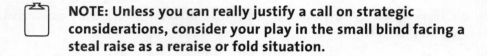 **NOTE: Unless you can really justify a call on strategic considerations, consider your play in the small blind facing a steal raise as a reraise or fold situation.**

Play from the big blind

Since there are three things the small blind can do, we will cover them as follows:

♠ The small blind folds.

♠ The small blind calls.

♠ The small blind reraises.

The small blind folds

As the big blind, you face a simple decision to play heads-up with the steal raiser or not. If you decide to play, you can choose to reraise. Note you are looking at pot odds of 3-point-something to one, depending on the size of the small blind.

Even though out of position, you can play a reasonable number of hands here. In general, call (at least) with any hand you would have raised pre-flop in the cut-off. You have only one opponent, and he presumably has a suspect hand. Unless the button is extremely tight, never throw away a pair or any two Broadway cards. I do not recommend playing ace-rag, but you may play it if suited. Aside from that, I urge you to avoid big-little holdings, including the seemingly popular king-rag suited.

You may be thinking, "suited does not help you that much when you are heads-up." True, but there will be betting after the flop, and suited cards sometimes give you "the right to be aggressive." Post-flop betting in a heads-up situation often comes down to who can be more aggressive. It is harder for you to be more aggressive than the guy in position, but draws, sometimes even backdoor draws, permit a measure of aggression that will win a few extra pots for you when you don't flop a pair or better. And once in a while you'll make a draw and win a decent-sized pot.

Understanding that, also play suited connectors down to 7-6 suited. These hands play poorly in a heads-up showdown, but allow for aggression and sometimes hit big hands. As always, you need excellent judgment to play hands like this, as well as unsuited connecting cards down to 8-7, and one-gappers to 10-8. If your opponent is tough, or you are uncomfortable, folding these hands and giving up your blind is a reasonable option.

Given that you now know when to play and when to fold, which hands should you reraise with? My answer is (and some good players will disagree) usually very few. Your opponent is in position and will bet virtually every flop, so if you call the pre-flop raise, you will always get another chance to raise once you have more information. If your opponent is highly aggressive, wait for the turn to raise him with both excellent hands and bluffs.

If you think reraising pre-flop will somehow psychologically slow down the frequency of steal raises you see, then go ahead and do it more often. Three-betting pre-flop and betting the flop might induce more folds from your opponent than calling and check-raising the flop. The pots odds will be the same for him, but psychologically your opponent is more likely to call once he has bet after the flop. If your opponent is like this, you may find more success in reraising pre-flop. In a tight game, when your opponent is taking frequent shots at your blinds, vary your raising patterns depending on the response you want.

The small blind calls

The small blind probably should not have called, but he may not have read this book. His call implies he is not highly skilled at this phase of the game, so you do not have to tighten your standards on that score. However, if the small blind is the type of player who loves to lead at many flops, play fewer hands so you don't get sandwiched between the small blind and the original raiser.

His call improves your pot odds, which now become 5-to-1, thus increasing slightly the number of hands you can play, particularly drawing hands like suited connectors and suited single-gappers.

It also increases the incentive to raise, as now you will be getting two extra bets pre-flop for each one you put in. Unlike the heads-up case, these bets may not be available later, as one of the players may fold after the flop. In addition, with three players in the pot, there is slightly more incentive for the pre-flop raiser to check occasionally.

Reraise with your better hands, large pairs, and big aces. Nobody will fold for this raise, but with the steal raiser having questionable values, and the small blind (unless he is a very tough and experienced player) feeling too weak to reraise, you probably are getting your money in with a significant edge.

The small blind raises

This is always a tough situation for the big blind, which is one of the reasons it is such a good raise by the small blind. Not only is this the worst pot odds situation of the three scenarios (you are getting only 3-to-1), but also you may get raised again. If you play in a place where five bets is a cap, you have to worry about two more potential raises.

You may feel that both players are ganging up on you to take your blind away, and you could easily be right. But the price of poker has risen, and you simply cannot play mediocre hands just because each of your opponents may be weaker than normal raisers. In fact, we are back to the case that you primarily must raise or fold.

Making it four bets can be especially effective because the steal raiser may have simply been taking a shot, and may not be inclined to play for two more bets. All he was trying to do was quietly win a bit of money, not get involved in a raising war. If you can eliminate the steal raiser at least 10% of the time and create dead money, it is worth considerable equity to you.

If you are certain that the raiser will call, you can call with the lower range of hands you might play (A-10 suited, for example). But most of the hands you will play for two more bets are premium hands, and you should not be afraid to put in an extra raise with them.

You typically do not want to play drawing hands for extra bets in a short-handed situation. You can no longer rely as much on your opponents missing the flop, because there are now two of them. Play only hands you would open-raise with in early middle position, and make sure you reraise with them.

Playing after a non-steal raise

Steal raises are annoying, and you have to deal with them, but you will face a standard raise more frequently. This discussion is limited to a single raise.

Be selective against a raise no matter where it comes from. Think about the likely strength of the raiser's hand and your relative position after the flop to determine your playing criteria.

There are so many possible ways for the play to develop that I can't be comprehensive, but examining nine typical cases will give you a good idea how to play your blinds:

1. An early position player raises, and no one calls.
2. An early position player raises, and one person calls.
3. An early position player raises, and several players call.
4. A middle position player raises, and no one calls.
5. A middle position player raises after a player has called.
6. A middle position player raises, and several players call.
7. A late position player raises after one player has called.
8. A late position player raises after several players have called.
9. The button raises after the cut-off calls.

1. An early position player raises, and no one calls

If you are ever going to play tightly in the blinds, this is the moment. You are out of position against a player who has announced a premium hand. If you are new to the game, you might think, "I don't know this guy, maybe he raises more often than he should." If that were the case, someone else would probably have called or three-bet.

The fact that everyone folded should tell you this is not the time to venture forth with a mediocre or poor holding. This is especially true if you hold an ace. In this exact situation, fold A-J automatically, and frequently fold A-Q as well. Small pocket pairs might be playable if you know the player is predictable (he will bet the flop and check the turn with a big ace, and bet the turn with a big pair). If you are going to play a small pair out of the small blind, though, you need to reraise to protect your pair from overcards in the big blind, who will be tempted to call because you just made the pot bigger.

2. An early position player raises, and one person calls

Even though you are now out of position to two players, you can play a few more hands. Not only is the pot bigger, but the EP raiser will play more honestly because of the additional player. Thus, it will be easier to tell where you are. Bad aces play especially poorly here, even when suited, because if the raiser does not have a good ace, the caller might. Never play a bad ace here. There is less reason to reraise from the small blind with a small to medium pair, as the extra player has already created too many overcards, and you will be primarily fishing for a set. Big cards are dangerous, but you can see a flop with suited connectors if you have the discipline to fold when you flop an underpair and decide it is a loser.

3. An early position player raises, and several players call

You can call with your volume hands, but avoid big-little combinations (e.g., K-6, A-4). You can play suited aces, but beware of playing if you flop a pair; you are looking for a flush draw or a miracle flop such as trips.

One of the reasons you can play more hands is that most of the time the pre-flop raiser will bet. Since he is on your left, you will have excellent relative position for the first and possibly subsequent betting rounds. Thus, you can see what the others do before committing yourself.

4. A middle position player raises, and no one calls

Compared to the early raiser case, a middle position raiser will have a greater variety of hands. As a result, the blinds can play more hands. Actually, I recommend that you fold the small blind with all but premium hands, as you are still in a raise or fold situation, but you are more likely facing a real hand rather than a steal.

The big blind can add suited aces as well as K-Q and K-J as they are less likely to be dominated here.

5. A middle position player raises after a player has called

I have included this case because this raise has some interesting characteristics. It can't be a steal raise as there is no hope of winning the blinds without a contest (the limper will call). But it could be an isolation raise made with mediocre values if the limper is a weak player, and the raiser knows this and is exploiting his weakness.

If this is the case, either blind can make a play with a decent hand by reraising. This may get the limper (and the big blind if the small blind reraises) to fold, create dead money, and take the initiative away from the raiser who was just making a play. Note this is a dangerous play, as the raiser might not be making an isolation raise and may just have a premium hand. You really need to know the players to try this. If not, simply play as if the middle position player had open-raised.

6. A middle position player raises, and several players call

You can treat this case much the same as if the raise came from early position. Your relative position will be good after the flop, and the raiser should play honestly because of the callers behind him.

7. A late position player raises after one player has called

All of the comments about isolation plays hold true here, probably even more so. Late position raisers take all sorts of liberties with raises, especially if they do not respect the limper. Again, you can play a lot of hands here, but if you are going to play, give serious thought to reraising. It can still show a long-term profit if you play well by creating dead money and gaining the initiative in case everyone misses the flop. You will be playing out of position and, especially if the caller does not fold to your three-bet, you will have to proceed cautiously.

8. A late position player raises after several players have called

Surprisingly, this is not as good a situation for you as the one where an early position player raised, and there were several callers. First, you will not be last to act, and there may well be more raising. Second, if form holds, everyone will check to the raiser on the flop, and he will bet. That will put you in terrible relative position, acting before the entire field. Thus, you should play only very good hands, and I do not recommend unsuited small cards even if they are connected. Play suited connectors down to 6-5s, but you will need to hit the flop quite solidly to continue. Play all pocket pairs.

9. The button raises after the cut-off calls

This is an extreme case of likely isolation. You should reraise with any hand you are going to play in either blind. The cut-off clearly has a mediocre hand and is likely a weak player, as he did not open-raise in late position. The button has no fear of someone waking up with a hand behind him, and his raise could simply be a combination isolation/steal. Still fold mediocre hands, but three-bet any hand with good high card strength.

Playing the small blind with no raise

Often, you find yourself in one of the blinds when there has been no raise. We will start with the small blind. When should you fold, call, or raise from the small blind?

Even though it has an effect on the decisions you would make in the situations we have covered previously, I have avoided discussing the size of the small blind to keep a complex subject under control. We need to look at that now.

Four factors enter into your decision on how to play. In no particular order, these are:

1. The size of the small blind.
2. The big blind's raising tendencies.
3. Your hand.
4. The number of pre-flop callers.

1. The size of the small blind

In most limit games the small blind is one-half the size of the big blind. When half the big blind would be a fractional number of chips, casinos select a number totaling either one-third or two-thirds the big blind. Most low-limit games use one-third (in a $3-$6 game, the small blind is $1), and higher-limit games use two-thirds (in a $15-$30 game, the small blind is $10), but there is no standard rule. In any case, how much more you need to put in definitely affects your decision of whether to complete the bet if no one has raised. Obviously, the more money you have already committed, the more likely you are to complete, but you also need to take the other factors into account before making your decision.

2. The big blind's raising tendencies

Often overlooked is how likely the big blind is to raise. Most big blind players are quite passive, but some love to raise whether we think they are correct or not. If the big blind is a significant threat to raise behind you, be prepared to muck many of your weaker hands that you would otherwise like to play.

3. Your hand

Of course, you need to consider your hand. We will discuss hand types and how to play them as we go through the possible scenarios.

4. The number of pre-flop callers

The final major factor in your decision is the number of players who have called pre-flop and to some extent their position. We will examine these cases:

- ♠ One player has called.
- ♠ Two or three players have called.
- ♠ Four or more players have called.

One player has called

To me, this is the most interesting case. The pot is quite small, but there is only one voluntary player, and he has shown no real strength. With any hand of quality (pair, two Broadway cards, any ace, suited connectors down to 8-7s), you should raise. You intend to create dead money by eliminating the big blind as often as possible, allowing you to play heads-up with the lead against the player with the weak hand. Even if he holds a better hand than you, your aggression will still win a lot of pots if the big blind folds, and you both miss the flop, as happens frequently. If the big blind calls or reraises, and you miss the flop, you can always give up on the hand and avoid sustaining a big loss. This raise from the small blind is yet another *Illusion of Action* opportunity, as a raise from out of position with a hand like 10-9 suited will look foolish to many opponents.

If the big blind "defends" all of the time, you should simply complete with your weaker aces, small pairs and suited connectors. In general, though, if you are unwilling to raise with your hand here, you should throw it away unless you have already put in two-thirds of a bet, and the big blind almost never raises.

Two or three players have called

You still want to raise with your best hands, such as A-A, K-K, Q-Q, and A-K suited. If you feel you can eliminate the big blind, you can raise with A-K, A-Q, and A-J as well. The advantage to raising is that you almost certainly have the best hand, and should be willing to build a pot. The disadvantage of raising with A-K, A-Q, or A-J, is that you lose your strategic advantage to bet, check-raise the flop, or check-raise the turn, depending on how you like the flop and how your opponents play.

If you have raised, you will almost always lead whether you hit or miss the flop. This leads to your playing out of position without being able to read and evaluate your opponents' actions. I prefer to play strategically after the flop with a well-disguised hand rather than bashing pre-flop out of position and recommend frequently completing the small blind with all but the top four hands listed above.

If you do not have a premium hand, generally proceed as follows:

- ♠ With two-thirds of a bet in, complete with any two cards.
- ♠ With half a bet in, complete with pairs, any two suited, all one- and two-gappers.
- ♠ With one-third of a bet in, complete only if you have a hand you would normally play in late position.

Four or more players have called

Now we have a multiway pot, with you and the big blind making at least six-way action. You should still raise with A-A and K-K because these powerful hands have such a premium over the field that you should be willing to build a pot any time you see them.

You also need to think about building a pot on some volume hands. The best among these are pairs below jacks. If you are going to have five or more opponents, you should usually raise with smaller pairs. You will still typically check and fold after the flop if you miss your set, but when you do hit a set, you would like to have your opponents tied into a larger pot and chasing with one-pair hands or overcards while drawing nearly dead.

In addition, playing a set does not have the positional disadvantages that one-pair and drawing hands do. (While position always matters, a set is such a powerful hand that your actions are easier to determine and less dependent on the other players' actions.) Once again, this small blind raise with a hand like 5-5 confuses opponents, and provides another opportunity for the *Illusion of Action.*

For variety, balance, and image, also raise with K-Q suited, Q-J suited and J-10 suited occasionally. This also provides *Illusion of Action* to your game, as opponents will see you are not just raising out of the small blind with only big pairs. These hands are sometimes difficult to play after the flop out of position, so if you are not experienced, make this play more sparingly.

If you do not have one of these combinations, you are still going to play many hands here.

- ♠ With two-thirds of a bet in, complete with any two cards.
- ♠ With half a bet in, complete with all but your worst hands.
- ♠ With one-third of a bet in, complete only if you have a normally playable hand.

Playing the big blind with no raise

It's always nice to get a free play in the big blind, but sometimes you should raise instead of just checking. Let's look at these by the number of opponents you are facing.

Against only one limper your raises should be determined primarily by the limper's standards and how well he plays. You can raise fairly liberally against most players if you feel you have the best hand, especially if the opponent is passive and will not always bet the flop for you.

I want to consider as a special case the times you are against one limper plus the small blind. You should go out of your way to raise if you feel the small blind will fold part of the time. Many small blind players who put in only one-third of a bet will fold to a raise, but few who put in two-thirds will. Take that difference into account.

Raising with your better high-card hands (A-K through A-9, K-Q through K-10, pairs) forces a small blind who has a weak hand and tossed in half a bet to commit another full small bet or fold. Most small blinds will continue to put money in the pot even with trash, but the advantage you have over him is great and worth the raise.

Against two or three players, raise only with your top pairs, A-K and A-Q. You are not getting the volume to make fancy raises with drawing hands, and your post-flop position is worse with more players in.

Against four players (one of them may be the small blind), raise only with top pairs. Do not raise with A-K or worse, as big cards play poorly against a larger field, which this has now become. A-K does not play well out of position multiway, particularly the two times out of three that you miss the flop. When you do hit an ace or king, your raise may discourage action you might otherwise get. Many late position players will bet into an A-x-x or K-x-x board with anything if you check to them, hoping to pick up the pot without a fight, so you will frequently get a chance to check-raise when you do hit your hand.

With five or more limpers you can raise with a large number of volume hands as well as classic power hands. You should still always raise with A-A and K-K. With Q-Q, J-J and perhaps 10-10 simply check. You have enough high card value that you will occasionally flop an overpair, and when you do, you want to be able to check-raise to protect your hand from overcard callers. Plus, you will get calls from players who do not suspect a hand this good.

With pairs below tens raising make sense. You are now unlikely to flop an overpair, but you are still getting an excellent price to hit your set. If you do flop a set, you want the pot large so people with overcards and one-pair hands will stay in, hoping to catch something to beat you while drawing nearly dead. If you make this raise, do not continue to put money in the pot unless you hit your set or an overpair. Don't try to bluff your way though a large field because you made a pre-flop raise.

You can also raise here with A-K suited and K-Q suited. These have high card value (chances are your opponents do not hold A-K or A-Q since there was no raise) as well as volume value if two cards of your suit hit. These hybrid hands offer a combination of possibly having the best hand and flopping a big draw, making it worthwhile to increase the size of the pot. Do not raise if your A-K or K-Q is not suited, for the reasons discussed above in the four-handed case.

A final hand for occasional raises is J-10 suited. This hand plays well in volume pots as it has excellent straight possibilities as well as flush potential. This is a powerful drawing hand, as J-10 makes the maximum number of straights, and when you do make a straight with a J-10, it is always the nut straight. Again, if you flop nothing, be prepared to check and fold.

Making these volume-hand raises in six-way or larger pots increases your volatility, so make them only if your bankroll and tolerance for volatility can sustain significant swings. A benefit of making these raises, in addition to long-term profit, is that they create *Illusion of Action* scenarios, confusing opponents who then give you excess action when you do raise with A-A or K-K.

Blind vs. blind

I never chop blinds, and typically I think you should not also. Online, you can't chop. So how should you play? Much depends on the relative skills of the players, and we don't have room here for a full discussion of heads-up play, but I do want to make a few observations.

If you are the small blind, the hands you play and how you play them depend on how well the big blind plays. If he is a weak, timid, or predictable player, you can play almost all of your hands, and you can raise with any ace, any two Broadway cards, and all pairs. If the big blind is a good, tough, or aggressive player, however, you should fold most of your hands and raise less with your good ones, hoping to trap later if you hit the flop or hold a premium hand. If you don't know anything about the big blind, err on the side of caution.

If you are the big blind and the small blind calls, raise with most normally playable hands. You have positional advantage and probably the best hand as well. If the small blind raises, you have to decide what sort of player he is. If he is tight, fold any hand you would not open-raise in middle position. If he is aggressive and raises a lot (some small blinds raise with anything), you should call with at least any ace, king, suited queen, pair, suited connectors higher than 5-4, Q-J through Q-8, and J-10 through J-7, and reraise with any pair or two high cards. You cannot afford to let an aggressive small blind take control of the action.

If your image is good, you can try a "programmed play" against an aggressive small blind. This is a play you decide to make before you see your cards or the flop. In this case, you call the raise, call the flop, and raise the turn. It is difficult for the small blind to call unless he has a really good hand, and if he is raising your big blind with any two, most of the time you will take the pot right there. As in all situational plays, use this sparingly, and expect that it will increase your volatility. Sometimes you will run into a big hand and lose many chips you did not even need to venture if you actually played your hand.

Playing trash hands out of the blinds

I want to mention blind hands that players would never play from any position unless they got a free play in the blind. They become lost when they are playing J♥-3♦ with four or five opponents and flop comes J♠-7♦-5♦. Should they bet out to avoid giving a free card? Check and try for the check-raise? Check and fold?

If you are an excellent player with good judgment, you may have a good feel for how to play hands like this. Otherwise, I suggest you use my rule of thumb: If you have a trash hand in a multiway pot, check and fold if there is any significant action unless you hit the flop twice. In the case of the J-3, that means if the flop does not come J-J-x, 3-3-x or J-3-x, check and fold if there is a bet and a call. Since one of your goals should be to avoid large losses with hands you would never play unless you were in the blind and nobody raised, missing an occasional opportunity to win a small pot should not bother you (it's hard to win a large pot with J-3 and a J-high board).

Conclusion

Do not be seduced by the fact that you can see flops cheaply if you have a terrible hand. Playing a hand out of position is difficult, and playing a bad hand out of position is even more so.

Remember that you still have options, and you must consider the number of players, the skill of the players, and the impact of your plays on future streets before deciding to complete, call, raise, or fold. Selective-aggressive play is the key to winning poker, and it still holds true when you are in the blinds.

Everyone loses money in the blinds, but with prudent play and right measure of aggression, you can lose a lot less than the other guys.

Part Two: Stages

On the Flop

Chapter Fourteen

Post-flop Planning

When you are in early position before the flop, you are really in the dark. All you know about the players to act after you is that they have two cards.

After the flop, even if you are first to act, you have far more information. You saw the action before the flop and have some idea what it means. The better you know how the opponents play and what they raise with or call with, the better judgment you can make. But before you act, you should estimate not only where you stand, but what is likely to happen.

Judge the probabilities that you have the best hand and/or a reasonable draw. Also, estimate how the hand will play out. Using that information, make a plan.

Planning is critical to success. Before you act, you should know what you are trying to accomplish with your play. Are you trying to win the pot right away? Protect your hand? Gain information? Bluff? Build a pot? Trap a bad player? Get a cheap draw?

After setting your goal, establish a plan to achieve it. Ask yourself: What is the best way to meet this objective? Consider the alternatives and select what you believe will be the best play. Then do it!

 NOTE: You should always know *why* you bet, or checked, or called, or raised.

Your plan must be fluid, and may even be way off the mark, but having some idea where you are and what you are trying to accomplish is critical to making and saving bets.

Here are some factors to consider when planning:

- ♠ Number of opponents
- ♠ How they play
- ♠ Nature of the flop
- ♠ The size of the pot
- ♠ Opponents' likely hands
- ♠ Your position
- ♠ Your hand

Number of opponents

If you have multiple opponents, the chances that someone has a small to very large piece of the flop go up considerably. Against one opponent, that chance goes down. Of course, you may not have much either.

In addition, more opponents means that the average winning hand goes up, since there are more ways for everyone to make hands. Let's look at some examples.

Example 1

You hold A♦-10♣, and see a flop of J♥-10♠-8♠. If you are against one player, you have an excellent chance to have the best hand. Play aggressively, as there are many draws your opponent could have. If you are against five opponents, almost always plan to give up. Not only are there decent chances you are already beat, but any king, queen, nine, eight, seven or spade will put your hand in jeopardy even if you happen to be leading. Moreover, a hand like A-J could easily dominate yours, so hitting your kicker could cost you a lot of money. Notwithstanding these risks, the size of the pot and the odds you are getting to continue still dominate. If you are getting the right price, you have to continue.

Example 2

You hold 9♦-9♠ and see a flop of J♥-8♣-3♦. Against one opponent, you likely have the best hand. Against seven opponents, you probably don't, and you are probably not getting the correct price to continue. Especially if there is much action, you should fold.

Example 3

You hold A♦-6♦ and play in the small blind. The flop is A♥-9♥-4♠. Heads-up your pair of aces has a good chance to be best. In a five-way pot, especially if there has been a raise and a call, you are swimming upstream with a small kicker and should give up.

Example 4

You hold 8♦-7♦ and see a flop of A♣-6♦-3♦. If there is one opponent, you will rarely be getting the right price to play this hand, though it may present semi-bluffing opportunities. If there are several opponents, you will be getting terrific odds to continue and will generally be going to the river to see if you can make your flush.

How they play

To some extent your plan will depend on how your opponents play. It is easier to play against predictable opponents and passive ones. Predictable ones often will let you know right away if you are ahead or behind. Timid players can be bullied or played for free cards.

If you face predictably aggressive opponents, you can decide to play off them, allowing them to take the lead, or get them to help you by raising to thin the field.

Example 1

You hold A♠-J♠ in the big blind. Someone open-raises in middle position, everyone folds, and you call. The flop is A♥-J♦-3♠, giving you the top two pair and a backdoor flush draw. How you should play this hand depends somewhat on how your opponent plays. Against a passive, calling opponent who will nevertheless bet the flop, try to check-raise the flop and bet the turn and river. Against an aggressive opponent, you might want to bet out, expecting him to raise with most hands and allowing you to three-bet. If he is very aggressive, you may even try for a check-raise later on in the hand.

Example 2

You hold 9♠-7♠ in late position and call two middle position limpers. Both blinds play. The flop is A♠-8♠-5♣, giving you a flush draw and a gutshot straight draw. Everyone checks to you. Against average players, you want to bet, hoping either everyone folds, two or more people call, or, if you miss your draw you get a free card on the turn. If there are some tricky or aggressive players in the hand, check and take the free card now while it's offered. You do not want to get check-raised and bet into on the turn, especially if the check-raise comes from a blind and knocks out the remaining players.

I have included this last example for another reason. If you bet, you will probably come out fine, as there are only a few ways for the hand to go badly. You have 12 outs, and will be happy if you get two callers, or if you can get a free card on the turn. But even though it will work most of the time, you would still be "gambling" that the few unfortunate things (getting check-raised and heads-up, getting check-raised and three-bet, having someone bet the turn) will not happen. Clearly you need to improve to win. Take the free card now. You may even get another one.

Nature of the flop

Evaluate how many draws appear on the flop and how plausible the draws are. A flop like Q-J-8 is considerably more dangerous than a flop like 6-5-2, even though those are the same gap and distance. Chances are that Q-J-8 has hit a lot more typical players than 6-5-2 would. If you are holding A-8 in the first case and A-2 in the second case, your A-8 is practically worthless, while your A-2 could easily be the best hand.

Big drawing flops make players want to raise and reraise. You need to anticipate this to make sure you are not caught in the crossfire.

Example

You hold A♥-J♠. You open-raise and are called by three players behind you and the big blind. The flop hits J♦-10♦-9♠. The big blinds bets out, and you are next to act. You should fold. You have top pair top kicker, but only the remotest redraws. The chances that one pair will win this pot are very small. Worse, you will probably have to put in many more bets just to see the turn, as it is highly likely that at least one player will raise on this two-pair, straight-draw-flush-draw board. You will have to pay too much when you do not have the best hand, and if you do hold the best hand, more than half the remaining deck will make you unhappy (nine diamonds, three tens, two nines, three eights, three sevens, three queens, and three kings equals 26 bad cards). Far too many players call or even raise in this position, only to be forced to put in two more bets on the flop. They then complain about the bad beat later in the hand, assuming that they were ahead to begin with.

The size of the pot

If I were writing a beginner's book, I would put this topic first. Pot odds and implied odds should always dominate your thinking. I list it here because I assume you already think about this. If you do not already know how many bets are in the pot when it is your turn, please start counting them immediately. Poker revolves around positive expectation, and if you do not know the reward, you cannot compute the risk-reward ratio.

If the pot is small, you may be able to steal more often, but you must also play fewer draws and longshots. You may also wish to take chances to increase the size of the pot.

Example

Here is a hand that exemplifies this principle. I was the big blind with K♣-J♣. In the small blind an aggressive and very tricky player raised after everyone had folded. From previous play, this meant he had something better than pure trash, but the range of possible hands was still very large. I reraised with my excellent heads-up hand and position.

The flop came K♦-3♥-3♠ and he checked. Of course, I might have been behind if he had A-A, K-K, A-K, or K-Q (or anything with a three), but I thought I was probably far ahead. In fact, if I bet, I would win the pot immediately most of the time. While I like winning pots as much as the next guy, I also felt that, if I checked, he would probably bet any hand he held trying to bluff me out. So I checked to give him a chance to bluff off some money.

The turn was the 10♥, making all sorts of draws possible. Sure enough, he bet, and I had to figure whether to raise or just call. I decided there were three possibilities:

- ♠ He had the best hand,
- ♠ He had picked up a draw, or
- ♠ He was flat out bluffing.

If he were ahead, calling would be far better than raising. If he was on a draw or had a worse made hand, I should probably raise, and if he was bluffing, I should clearly call.

Calling seemed better than raising for many cases, but there was even a more compelling reason to call. Since the board looked like many draws had developed, my opponent would probably interpret my call as meaning that I had picked up a draw. If he thought that, he would probably bluff the river with all of his pure bluffs and most of his missed semi-bluffs, hoping that I had missed my draw and would fold. I was not about to fold, so I would frequently pick up an extra big bet on the river as well as the one I had just picked up on the turn.

The river was a good news/bad news J♥, making the board K♠-3♥-3♦-10♥-J♥. I had made top two pair, but all sorts of straight and flush draws had got there. Again he bet and I called. Even though my hand improved on the river, a raise would serve no purpose, since my opponent would almost certainly fold any worse hand and would call or raise with better hands. He turned over the Q♦-9♦ for the straight and took the pot.

Let's look at the specific situation in which my opponent held Q♦-9♦. He almost certainly would have folded if I had bet on the flop, so I would always win the three big bets in the pot. Assuming we played this situation 15 times (for reasons what will be clear soon), I would be plus 45 big bets by betting the flop.

After I checked and the 10♥ came, my opponent now bet. Notice he put a full big bet into a pot that contained only three bets when his chances of making his hand were just under 14-to-1. He needed a jack to beat me, and I had one so there were three left in the deck out of 44 unknown cards. Thus he was a 41-to-3 dog, about 14-to-1.

In other words, my checking the flop convinced him as a 14-to-1 dog to put a full bet into a three-bet pot. Since I know I will call, he is taking 4-to-1 odds on a 14-to-1 event. Let's see how that turns out.

If we play this situation 15 times, he will win 5 big bets one time (I will always pay him off at the river), and lose *at least* one big bet fourteen times. Assuming he never bluffs the river when he misses, I win 4 bets 14 times (56 bets) and lose 5 bets once for a total of 51 bets, compared to the 45 I would win if I bet on the flop. My check nets 6 bets over 15 hands. Moreover, if he bluffs half the times he misses (and I expect him to bluff more than that), I would win another seven big bets on top of that! That would make a total of 13 bets I will additionally win.

By offering him the chance to overpay greatly for his draw, I earn almost a full bet on every single hand when he holds exactly what he did hold.

TIP: When the pot is small, you gain tremendously if you induce your opponent to put money in with terrible odds, even though he sometimes gets there.

Example

Here is another example, one that I actually won. In a game in which I had a loose image (which as you now know I cultivate, while still trying to play tight), I open-raised on the button with Q♠-9♥. The small blind, who had shown signs of tiring of my aggressive play, called me. He checked the flop of Q♥-J♦-4♣. Even though the flop had many draws, I decided to check behind him to encourage action. I thought this would be a good play in part because a few rounds earlier, I had raised, then checked and folded in a similar situation when I flopped nothing on a dangerous board.

I risked a free card to possibly gain a few bets in a small pot. He checked again when the 5♣ came on the turn, I bet and he check-raised! Because I had misrepresented my hand on the flop, I was committed to calling all the way to the river, not knowing if his check-raise was in response to my deception, or he had a big hand. I called the raise, and the river when an 8♦ came. He showed down A-5, so I won three additional big bets over what I probably would have won had I bet the flop.

TIP: Gambling to gain extra bets in small pots when you have the lead can often gain you more bets than the whole pot was worth originally.

If the pot is large, stealing becomes harder, though much more profitable.

Protecting the pot by eliminating opponents and even distorting your betting to look for chances to limit the field must become part of your plan.

Example

You have A♣-A♦ in the big blind. After four players and the small blind call, you (correctly) raise. Everyone calls, as you expected. The flop is K♦-10♣-8♥. Chances are you are ahead, and you certainly do not want to give a free card. However, the board is filled with gutshot possibilities as well as open-ended straight possibilities. You can't do much about the open-ended draws, but you may be able to do something about the gutshots. If you bet out, the next player will be getting 13-to-1, which is more than enough to take one off for the 11-to-1 gutshot on the turn.

Because the pot is large, you need to take some extra risk to try to eliminate these draws, or at least to give them much worse odds. Even though you probably have the best hand and were the pre-flop raiser, you should check and hope a late position player bets so you can check-raise, presenting the rest of the field with 7.5-to-1 odds instead of 13-to-1. In fact, it would be nicer if a late position player bet and another raised so you could put in a third bet and really narrow the opposition. You could easily still have the best hand, since a likely bet-raise to you would be a straight draw and a king.

What if everyone checks, and someone hits his gutshot? He may thank you for the free card and even offer you a lecture about the folly of your poor play, but the reality is that he was not going to fold anyway so this was a hand you were destined to lose. And if everyone checks, and a blank hits the turn, you can bet and offer the next player only 7-to-1 because you are now making a big bet.

Remember, it was both the large pot and the presence of multiple possible gutshots that convinced you to play this way. If the flop had been 9♥-3♦-2♣, you should just bet out.

Opponents' likely hands

You must do some detective work here. Your opponents have already done something to get to the flop: raised, called a raise, limped (which means they had the opportunity to raise and did not), or reraised. All their actions had meanings.

Some had more meaning than others. If your very tight opponent limped under-the-gun, you can put him on a narrow range of hands: perhaps, 10-10, 9-9, 8-8, A-Q, A-J, K-Q suited. If a middle position player open-raised, the range of hands you can assign him depends on how you have seen him play. Some players require a premium hand; some will have any ace, pocket pair, or any two Broadway cards. Very few will have a hand like 6-5 suited, and eventually you will learn who those few players are.

You job is to figure out how the flop may or may not fit with their likely hands based on their pre-flop betting. You can make only an approximation, but that is better than just saying to yourself, "Who knows what they have?" Use this estimate as a guideline when planning your play.

Example

A tight opponent raises, and you call in the blind with 9♣-9♠. The flop is K♥-6♥-2♣. You think about your opponent's likely hands, which you decide are A-A, K-K, Q-Q, J-J, 10-10, A-K, A-Q, and A-J. The only ones you can actually beat are A-Q and A-J. If you decide to do a count (as you should), you find that he has you beat 42 times (six each A-A though 10-10 and 12 A-Ks) and you are ahead 32 times (sixteen each for A-Q and A-J) which makes you a 4-to-3 dog. Even if you are ahead, he can still draw out. Plus you are out of position, so you cannot make extra bets in the event you are ahead.

Some of the times you are behind, however, he may be afraid of the king on the board, so that possibility must be considered. If he greatly respects your play, you may think about making a play for the pot, hoping he either has one of the hands you can beat, or he will lay down Q-Q, J-J, and 10-10 if you represent a king strongly enough. If he will never lay down a big pair, then making a play is useless. You are not getting the right price to play the hand and must check and fold when he bets.

Against a looser opponent, with a much broader range of hands, the likelihood that you are beat goes down considerably. If he can have any pocket pair, an ace, or several hands like Q-J and J-10, you cannot fold. How you decide to play will depend on:

- ♠ How predictable your opponent is,
- ♠ How you believe he will play hands when he is ahead, and
- ♠ How he will play when he is behind.

But you must do something, and you can't just check and fold when you are against a loose opponent. Determine your opponent's likely hands and how they fit with the board before developing your plan.

Your position

Think about your absolute and relative position. Your plan will depend on where you are and what you wish to accomplish. As I said earlier, all of your desired actions are easier if you are in position. Whether you want to build a pot, get a free card, protect your hand, or bluff, having the best position makes a big difference.

I have already discussed position quite a bit. In terms of post-flop planning, assess how to use your position to accomplish what you want. Can you improve your absolute position by raising and causing players behind you to fold? Can you gain reliable information by making a play now? Should you risk a bad card on the flop to be able to raise the turn and present opponents with a double big bet? Should you try for a free card?

NOTE: Position is not just something you have. It's something you must *exploit*.

Even if you are in early position, you still need to assess how to make the most of the position you have. Whatever you do, *do not check in the dark*. The next chapter will discuss reasons for this in detail.

Your hand

I list this last, but not because it's unimportant. Most players spend too much time thinking about their hand and too little thinking about the other factors. You need to think about your hand, of course, but also about what your opponents think your hand may be. Too many players give up excellent bluffing opportunities because they know what they have and forget that their opponents do not know.

Decide the probability that you have the best hand. If you do, then you must think about the best way to protect it if it is vulnerable, and the best way to maximize your win if it is powerful.

If you think you have the best hand, but are uncertain, then consider how to find out at the lowest cost while still protecting it.

Example

You also must think about the chances that you will have the best hand after two more cards come. If you hold A♦-A♠ and the flop is 10♥-9♥-8♥, there is a reasonable chance you have the best hand right now, but against six opponents, your chances of actually winning are fairly small. You cannot afford to see a queen, jack, ten, nine, eight, seven, six, or heart, and even a card like a king may give someone a likely two pair. If there is much action, your best course may be to fold immediately.

Frequently, the number of opponents will enter into your decision about whether your hand might be best. If you raise with A-K, and just the big blind calls, chances are a flop of J-8-5 did not hit him. You should proceed as if you hold the best hand. If five players call, the chances you have the best hand is small, and you should plan to check and fold. Of course, if the player to your left bets and gets a few callers and no raise, you will be getting 15-to-1 or better, and should take one off, alert to the danger that if you hit you may still lose.

If you do not have the best hand, you need to decide wheth... getting the right price to draw for it. Your assessment need... for your implied odds – the extra money you may make if yc... but also needs to include the chances that you will make you... ...u and still lose. If you have 5-4 and the board is 10-7-6, you have an open-ended straight draw, but an eight will make the board 6-7-8-10, and anyone with a nine will have you drawing dead to a three-out tie at best. In fact, you may already be drawing dead.

This subject is dealt with in great detail in Rolf Slotboom and Dew Mason's book, *Hold'em on the Come*, in which they detail ways to count outs and decide whether to keep on playing.

If you are unlikely to have the best hand, and you are not getting the right price for your draw, the only thing left before folding is to decide your chances of winning through a bluff. If you decide, based on the number of opponents, their tendencies, their likely holdings, your image, and the texture of the flop that a bluff has a positive EV, go ahead and try it. While this may be rare:

 TIP: You don't need to hold the best hand if you are not going to have to turn it over.

Example

You have 5♠-3♠ in the small blind. There is one middle position limper, you call, and the big blind checks. The flop hits A♦-K♣-8♠, giving you nothing at all. But there are very good chances that this flop has also missed the big blind (who has any two cards, but might have raised with a good ace), and the limper (who also may not have an ace or king). Even if he limped with a hand like J-10, giving him a gutshot straight, he would be getting only 4-to-1 if you bet. And with a hand like 7-7, he still would probably fold.

If you bet here, you need to win only one time in three to show a profit. Against the right players, you should make this play occasionally. If you make it constantly, opponents will realize you are just betting because it's your turn. The pot may seem too small to bother with, but that's also in the minds of your opponents. In fact, small pots are the easiest to steal because nobody cares that much about them. And 1½ big bets with no hand is a very nice pick-up.

Conclusion

Many people sort of "play at poker" rather than playing poker. When it is their turn to act, they guess at what to do, generally checking and calling. Playing correctly requires thinking about your hand, the board, and what you would do to minimize your loss or maximize your profit.

Certainly, you have to take into account what your opponents are doing, and what you think they are trying to accomplish as well. Your plans must be dynamic, changing as conditions and your opponents' actions dictate changes. Even if your plan is sometimes wrong, having one puts you way ahead of the average player, and as you improve, so will your results.

Chapter Fifteen

Reraising on the Flop

A frequent decision on the flop is how to deal with a raise. If you believe you are beat and are not getting the price to continue, you fold. If you think you getting the right price, call.

There are also times when you should reraise. They include:

- ♠ You have a big draw.
- ♠ You likely have the best hand.

You have a big draw

When you have a big draw, reraising will often get you at least current pot odds. By that I mean the odds you will make your draw are better than price you are getting on the current betting round. Here is an example.

Example

After two limpers, you raise from the cutoff with A♥-J♥. The button, big blind, and the limpers call. On the flop of K♥-8♥-7♣, three players check and you bet. The button raises, the big blind calls, as does one limper. Your reraise should be automatic. You have three opponents, so you getting 3-to-1 on your money *on this betting round* if you reraise and they all call. You are just a 2-to-1 underdog to make your flush by the river, and it is possible that an ace will also give you a winning hand. In other words, on this betting round, you are putting in 25 percent of the money and expecting to take out at least 33 percent of the money.

Some players do not reraise here because they realize they will lose two-thirds of the time. If you are among them, rethink your strategy. If you cannot afford or psychologically tolerate the volatility that comes from making obvious +EV plays, then play lower so you can. You can't be a significant winner if you allow opportunities like this one to pass you by.

You likely have the best hand

Sometimes you flop an excellent hand, such as two pair or better. In that case, you will have to make a decision whether to reraise on the flop or wait and raise the turn. If you are out of position, the decision is tougher because if you wait for the turn to check-raise, you may end up checking and not getting a chance to raise if everyone else checks as well.

Let's take a look at the factors that you should consider when making this decision to three-bet the flop, or attempt a check-raise on the turn.

1. How many opponents do you have?
2. How vulnerable is your hand?
3. Might the raiser want a free card?
4. Can a scare card come?
5. Who is the raiser?
6. What is your image?

1. How many opponents do you have?

The more opponents who are still in, the more likely you should be to three-bet on the flop. Many opponents stay in with longshot draws on the flop, planning to fold on the turn if they do not help. Collecting extra bets from them is typically worth more on the flop while they are still in to pay the raises. Even better, if there still opponents who have called only one bet so far, a reraise by you might get some of them to fold a hand that might draw out on you, potentially saving you the whole pot.

Conversely, if you are heads-up, the extra money can come only from collecting an additional large bet instead of an additional small one. While this difference should not dominate your thinking as much as the considerations below, it is extra money. If you can go for it, you should.

2. How vulnerable is your hand?

Having the best hand now does not mean you win the pot. You must still survive two more cards. If you feel you hand might not hold up, you might want to wait for the turn before raising to see if you still like your hand.

Example

You get a free play in the big blind with Q♦-4♣ and see a flop of Q♠-8♥-4♦. You bet out and are raised, which narrows the field down to the two of you. I would classify this hand as vulnerable, but you have to decide what the bad cards are. Clearly, an eight is terrible. It counterfeits your two pair leaving you with queens and eights. What else might be bad for you?

Typical middle-limit opponents in this situation would have raised before the flop with A-Q, called with K-Q and Q-J, and possibly have folded Q-10 or worse. This makes a king or jack potentially dangerous cards for you as well as the eight. It might be right in this case to call on the flop planning to check-raise if a danger card does not come, and check-call or even fold if a bad card for you does fall.

On the other hand, if you got the free play in the blind with Q♦-8♣ and bet out, three-bet right now. Trying for a check-raise might work also, but there are still chances that your opponent will check behind you (for reasons we will discuss). In addition, there is some chance your opponent will want to get into a betting war on the flop, which he rarely will want to do on the turn unless he has you beaten.

3. Might the raiser want a free card?

If you are going to wait for a check-raise, you need to be fairly sure your opponent will bet. The more draws the board presents, the more likely it is that your opponent is raising for a free card, and will not bet when you check to him. In this case, you must three-bet right now.

Example

If the board on your Q♦-4♣ hand were Q♠-9♠-4♥, you should probably three-bet instead of waiting to check-raise. (Some of you would prefer to call and bet out if a blank hits. That is another option, but the aggressive route of raising is more profitable in the long run.) There is just too much chance that if you call and check, you will give up a free card to a flush or straight draw.

4. Can a scare card come?

Another thing that might keep your opponent from betting the turn would be a scary turn. A meaningless card to both of your hands, but which looks like it might have hit you, could foil your check-raise plans.

Again, let's try an example.

Example

In the big blind with 8♥-7♥, you call a raise from a tight middle position opponent. The flop comes 8♦-7♣-2♠. You bet out and get raised, almost guaranteeing that this particular opponent has a big pair, because you know that he would call with overcards. There is probably nothing that can come on the turn that will deter this opponent from betting out, and you would be correct to wait and check-raise. Waiting becomes even more profitable when you consider that another deuce will counterfeit your hand and save you money if it does show up.

But suppose the flop were 8♦-7♣-6♥. You still have top two, and there is little chance that this particular opponent has any kind of straight draw (though he might have A-10, 10-10, or 9-9, these are remote and you should not change your play because he may have one of them). Now, however, if a five or nine comes, your opponent may be too scared to bet, so you will not get a chance to check-raise. In this case, then, you have to three-bet now or risk having your opponent shut down and give you no more action if the wrong turn card hits.

5. Who is the raiser?

As always, it helps to know who your opponent is and how he plays. Some players never make a free card raise, so you do not need to consider that. Some players are so aggressive that they will bet the turn every time if they raised the flop, regardless of what comes or why they raised in the first place. Against such players, you should almost always wait for the turn and check-raise.

Conversely, some opponents are very tricky and raise with all sorts of hands, hoping you will fold now, or they will get to see the river, and perhaps even call it, for one more big bet. Against these opponents, you must get your raise in now and take the lead.

6. What is your image?

Opponents take advantage of timid players by raising them frequently, because these timid players almost never play back. Typically they go immediately into check-and-call mode, unwilling to lay a hand down, but also unwilling to take any further aggressive acts without a near-nut holding.

If you are one of these timid players, or if you think you might be perceived as such, play back on the flop frequently. Do not wait for the turn. Your long-term success requires you to be seen as a force to be reckoned with.

Going into a protective shell whenever you get raised invites more and more players to raise you with impunity. After all, if you do not reraise occasionally, then the raiser figures at best you will fold or at worst you will check on the next street. You will encourage opponents to raise you, which is exactly the wrong thing to do.

When you can, you should three-bet on the flop with a good hand so people will not think they can run over you. Waiting for the turn, even when it works and you get to check-raise, will still not be seen as powerful as reraising now.

Making this decision about when to raise is easier when you have position over the raiser. You can be certain of getting at least one bet in even if he checks, so you can wait for the turn in more cases. All of the factors mentioned still play a part, but your opponent's aggression level is somewhat less important.

Summary

Deciding which play to make when you have a choice is often very complex. Rarely does a single consideration dominate, and you have to consider many factors very quickly. Few choices at hold'em are totally clear, and making the best decision in these repeating situations makes a lot of difference.

You have seen the factors that should enter your trade-off as you decide what to do. I will, however, offer a solution for those of you who do not want to think about such things (how did you get to the end of this chapter?), or for those who, after due consideration, do not see a clear answer emerging.

 TIP: When in doubt, put the money in *now*!

Chapter Sixteen

Checking in the Dark

One of the stupidest plays in poker is the blind check before the flop hits in limit hold'em. Many times the blind or the first player to act should lead into a pot. Note that a dark check on the turn is equally silly, but far fewer players do this.

Many players think, "Checking in the dark makes sense because if I check, somebody else will bet, and then I can respond to it." Frequently they are correct, but only after looking at the flop and deciding that checking is the best play. Sometimes betting out of position is very powerful or even necessary to win the money.

Here are some of those times:

- ♠ Keeping the right of first bluff.
- ♠ Leading for bluff credibility in future hands.
- ♠ Betting to protect your hand.
- ♠ Betting to gain a tell.
- ♠ Leading to set up a bluff.
- ♠ Attempting to get three bets in on the flop.
- ♠ Putting opponents in the middle.

Keeping the right of first bluff

In the hand at the end of Chapter 14 you held 5♠-3♠ in the small blind and led into a board of A♦-K♣-8♠, after one limper had come into the pot. If you decided to check in the dark, either the big blind or the limper would have bet in most middle-limit games. If you now decided to make a play for the pot, you would have to check-raise, putting in two bets to win four. So instead of betting, which would be profitable if it worked one time in three, you would have to win half the time to break even. Assuming the limper was the bettor, he would now be getting 6-to-1 for his call, and may even do so with hands as weak as the J-10 he would have folded to your flop bet. If he calls your check-raise, you have no idea how to proceed with your pure bluff.

By retaining the right to make the first move, you significantly improve your chances to pick up this orphan pot with little risk and reasonable odds.

Right of first bluff also happens when you see a flop with small cards, one of which is paired. If the flop is 7♣-7♥-3♦, you would like to be the first one to represent it, particularly if your opponents will fold rather than play on with hands like Q♠-J♠.

Leading for bluff credibility in future hands

Having a balanced approach is critical to establishing FUD. On that flop of 7♣-7♥-3♦, you should lead from the blind with hands like 5♣-5♦, 6♣-5♦, 8♥-8♦, 8♥-7♦, K♥-3♥, and sometimes Q♣-9♣.

Notice I included hands with sevens in them. Many players automatically check when they flop trips, thinking they should wait for the turn. Some of the time you should, but at least half the time you should bet. Against many opponents, some of them will call your flop bet with overcards, which is highly profitable for you because they are already drawing nearly dead. If you wait for the turn, they could miss and fold, limiting the money you can make.

Equally important, opponents may see that you actually have the hand you represented. If you play with these opponents often, you have now created FUD. Your opponents learn that sometimes your bet on a paired board means you have trips, and sometimes it means you have nothing. They won't know how to play against you and may decide simply to fold rather than tangle with you. Even if they play, their bets and raises will be more predictable, allowing you to read their hands more easily.

You cannot establish that credibility without leading at flops like this with trips. If you represent trips only when you don't have them, but never bet when you do have them, observant opponents will try to outplay you on later streets.

Betting to protect your hand

You have 9♦-9♠ in the big blind. An aggressive early position player raises before the flop. There are three callers and you call as well, making the pot ten small bets. The flop comes 8♠-6♣-3♦. If the early raiser doesn't have a big pair, your overpair is likely best. However, your hand is vulnerable to overcards, so you want to limit the field by making them face a raise. So what's your best play?

You can check-raise to build a pot, but that is not your objective. You want to get others to fold. The best chance for that is to bet and hope for cooperation from the original raiser. Since he is aggressive, he may raise with overcards, hoping to eliminate other players and get a free card from you on the turn. Yes, he will also raise with big pairs, but with the pot already large you can't give up just because there was a pre-flop raiser. By leading and getting raised, you both combine to create that dead money we all love. If you check in the dark, you have no chance to make this play and protect your hand.

Betting to gain a tell

Here's a little known fact about tell play that I use a great deal. I make it only when playing live because online it is useless.

Example

You have 7♣-7♥. There is a raise and two callers. You call in the blind. The flop is 9♣-6♥-2♦. The important thing to you is whether the raiser has a real hand or some overcards, and you would like to know that very quickly.

If you check to the raiser, he is going to bet. He will bet

comfortably because he knows your check is coming. He is confident that everyone will check to him, and he expects to bet. As a result, you learn nothing from his action. But if you bet, he is suddenly faced with a situation he was not expecting.

He has to make a surprise decision. He wasn't planning to make a decision. If he has a big pair, normally his decision is pretty easy: He's raising.

But what if he doesn't have a big pair? What if he has A-K or A-Q with a couple of players behind him, and now he has to decide: Should he raise and try to eliminate them? Should he fold because he's not drawing to any pure outs, and he may face a raise behind him? Should he call and try to hit one of his overcards? Often he hesitates, and that hesitation can be easy to read.

Some opponents automatically raise when you bet into them after they have raised pre-flop, so you can't learn much. You can use them to help you protect your hand. Others give you this great hesitation tell, but only if you fire right into them. If you check, you learn nothing.

Leading to set up a bluff

There is a wonderful variation play that can be used against the auto-raisers. But first, let's look at how you might play the previous hand on the turn.

You held 7♣-7♥, and after a raise and two callers, you called in the blind. The flop was 9♣-6♥-2♦. You correctly led, an auto-raiser raised, and the others folded. You decided to call to see the turn.

If the turn is not an ace, king or queen, you may want to bet again to prevent the auto-raiser from taking a free card. You bet will offer him 7-to-1, which is not enough to draw to six outs, especially since he will (reasonably) conclude that you may have two pair or a set, hands that leave him drawing dead. If he does have overcards, he will often fold, especially if you are known to bet hands like two pair on the turn rather than check-raising much of the time. If he raises, you will have a tough decision, but unless you know he is hyper-aggressive, you will often conclude that he really does have a big pair and fold.

Now assume you have J♥-9♥ and call a middle position raise from the big blind. You flop a flush draw with 6♥-4♥-2♣. You lead out hoping to win right now, but your opponent raises. You believe this could be a raise to take the lead, get a free card, and see the river for one big bet. Obviously, you would not mind seeing the river for one big bet either, but you also realize that if your opponent bets, you will be getting the right price to call. One approach would be to represent a big hand by three-betting and leading at the turn. This can be expensive, especially if you are raised again, but it also gets your opponent to fold on occasion.

I prefer the following play, which few players use. Call the raise and wait for the turn. If the turn does not help you, but also does not appear to help him, bet. You want a free card so I understand why checking is attractive, but betting here mimics the previous play where you had a made hand and wanted to prevent a free card. Your opponent is getting a worse price than before and will often fold overcards.

This is not just speculation. I have been using this double-lead-bet-with-a-draw play for several years with great success. I balance my game by making the same play with one pair, two-pair, and even straights and flushes.

The keys to this play are balance and the willingness to lead into the pre-flop raiser with a variety of hands. If you check dark, you will never be able to make this play.

Attempting to get three bets in on the flop

Your opponent raises before the flop, and you call from the blind. You flop a big hand, such as two pair or better. Check-raising on the flop is nice, but wouldn't it be better to get three bets in some of the time? If you check in the dark, that cannot happen unless your opponent is hyper-aggressive and decides to three-bet your check-raise, enabling you to raise again. This is rare, however, and generally you miss your chance to three-bet by checking in the dark.

The drawback to betting with a good hand, such as two pair or better, is that your opponent may fold, leaving you to collect only the pre-flop money. Check-raising may seem the better alternative, because it almost guarantees you at least one extra small bet, since the pre-flop raiser will almost certainly bet the flop when checked to.

While it is true that flop check-raisers will collect the extra small bet the vast majority of the time, there are distinct advantages to betting out, including those times your opponent is aggressive enough to raise anytime you bet.

Example

You hold A♠-10♠ in the big blind and call a middle position raise. The flop hits A♦-10♣-2♦. If he has a big ace, you want some action on this hand, and check-raising may kill it. If you bet out and he has A-K, A-Q or A-J, he may well raise, giving you a chance to three-bet. He may even raise with a big pair, thinking you may have a hand like J♦ 10♦, since he may figure that if you had a big hand, you would check-raise.

Putting opponents in the middle

Continuing with the example hand, you have A♠-10♠ again, but this time there are three limpers and then a raise. You call, as do the other players. If you bet out into the other players on that A♦-10♣-2♦ flop, you offer them 11-to-1 to hit a gutshot with a hand like K♣-Q♥, so it seems like they should call. But there is still the very real threat of a raise from the original raiser. If he raises, you will reraise. Let's say that one player calls, and now the original raiser does raise and you reraise. There are now 17 bets in the pot, and the caller must call two, giving him odds of 8.5-to-1, not nearly enough to go for an inside straight. Even if he calls and ends the raising, he will have put in a total of three bets for a current pot of 19 bets, meaning he will have paid 6.3-to-1 for his draw. If he folds to your reraise, you have created more dead money – an outcome that always makes you happy.

Aware opponents will recognize the danger someone may raise, and that they may be trapped for multiple bets with a hand like K♥-J♥. They would like to call one bet, but the threat of having to put in extra bets makes them fold.

Many opponents are "unaware one-bet-at-a-time types" who do not look ahead or think about what may happen. They will call, but if someone does raise and you do three-bet, they will either have to make a significant error by calling, or abandon the small bet they put in the pot.

Check-raising instead of betting has merit, but betting puts opponents under considerable pressure and ensures that someone (you) will bet. You do not want to check to the raiser and find that he is checking with a hand like 8♦-8♣.

This concept of putting your opponents into a position where they may be trapped comes up often. Most players who play one-bet-at-a-time poker get trapped, which is one of the reasons they lose. Players who visualize the next few possible plays may avoid these traps, but in doing so they must fold, creating dead money.

Conclusion

Most times that you are out of position, especially facing a pre-flop raise, you will check. Though the times you will want to bet will be few, they still exist, and only by seeing the flop and planning your play will you be able to decide which action is better.

Occasional betting gives your game balance, allows you to bluff at pots, increases your opponents' FUD factor, and allows you to trap opponents, get better reads, and get more money in the pot when you have a big hand.

Checking in the dark before you see the flop is simply voluntarily giving up one of the arrows in your quiver. It may not matter very often, but why would you give the enemy any unnecessary advantage? If poker is all about making good decisions, how good can your decisions be if you are making them in the dark?

Chapter Seventeen

Common Errors on the Flop

This chapter highlights three of the most common errors players make on the flop These errors, which are made every day in every game, are among the most costly that experienced players make. They include:

- ♠ Improper betting from the button.
- ♠ Raising with draws when next to act.
- ♠ Playing small pairs after the flop.

Improper betting from the button

We have all seen it many times. Five or so people see the flop. Everyone checks to the button, who bets. For a lot of players this bet is almost automatic. After all, everyone checked, so they think, "My opponents will all probably fold." In the tightest of games, everyone might fold on occasion, but in most games some players at least call, and a player who expected the button to bet will often check-raise.

Whether to bet or not depends on a number of factors, including:

- ♠ The quality of your hand (the better the hand, the more you should tend to bet).

♠ The number of opponents (the fewer there are, the more you should tend to bet).

♠ The texture of the flop (fewer draws make it more likely a bet will win).

♠ The nature of the players (tend to bet more often into passive players, less often into aggressive ones).

This is a difficult subject to deal with comprehensively, so I will try illustrating the thought process you need to have with one hand and four different flops. Assume you limp on the button with A♣-3♣ after three other players are in. The blinds also play, so there are five opponents. In all the cases below, they all check to you on the flop. Should you check or bet?

Flop 1: A♥-J♦-5♣

Clearly, you should bet this flop. You may easily have the best hand with your pair of aces. There are gutshot draws available (particularly K-10, Q-10, K-Q) and you should force these draws to pay for their 11-to-1 shot. The backdoor wheel draw and backdoor nut flush draw are also pluses for your hand, in case you get check-raised by a better ace.

Flop 2: Q♥-J♦-3♥

You have a pair with an overcard, and nobody bet, but this should be an easy check. Players who limp could easily have cards around this flop, there are multiple draws, and you could easily get check-raised. You are unlikely to win this pot with a pair of threes, and thus need to improve. You should check, planning to fold on the next round unless you improve. The best part is that when you do hit one of the five cards that will improve your hand, you will have position and a huge surprise for anyone who bets into you. Unless someone holds K-10, A-Q, or A-J, your two pair will be good. Players holding one of these hands might have bet the flop, but even if they would not, you can't worry about having a second-best hand if an ace comes. If you do, you will lose some extra bets.

Flop 3: A♦-8♠-3♥

Obviously, this is a wonderful flop for your hand. There is nothing wrong with a bet here, of course, but I still prefer a check. With no draws at all out there, you will get action only from another ace (or a player with an eight or a medium pair who thinks you may be bluffing). In a game where everyone calls the flop regardless of what they hold, a bet might be the best play. But in a game where people play well after the flop, a check here will be much more likely to make money. If someone makes something on the turn (even a draw), they might bet aggressively and let you get a raise in. If the flop was two-suited, or had a Broadway card in place of the eight, a bet would be mandatory.

Flop 4: Q♣-9♣-6♥

Again, many people bet here because they have a big draw and everyone checked. They hope that everyone folds, but they reason that even if they get two callers, they are getting a good price for their draw. All of this is true, but consider the opposite point of view. If someone bet and there was a caller, they might raise here for a free card, thus saving a small bet. But you can take the free card right now, and save a small bet just by checking. The best reason to bet is that you may get a better ace, such as A-10 to fold, thus giving you two more outs. If the pot was larger, this could be an excellent reason, but you do not need to protect extra outs in small pots as much as you do in big ones.

Just because you bet here does not mean you will get a free card on the turn. You could get check-raised now, or someone could decide to bet the turn. You are not going to win this hand unimproved, and there are several cards in the playing zone, so it is unlikely that everyone will fold. Also, consider that if you check here, you still might get another free card on the turn. While a bet is certainly reasonable, I prefer a check here.

We could construct thousands of cases, and that is what makes poker such a wonderful game of skill. A small difference in the flop could change the correct decision. But the moral of this segment is: Think before you bet on the button. Just because you have "something" does not mean a bet is the best action.

Raising with draws when next to act

The flop is something like K♦-10♠-4♦. A player bets into a field of five players. The next player, holding 8♦-7♦, raises. This play makes no sense, yet I still see it every day. Simply put, a draw wants company. You want lots of players in to give you the best price for your draw. You would not mind raising if four or five players were already in, since you rate to win a bit less than one time in three (even though you will make your flush more often than that, it might still lose).

Exceptions arise when the pot is large, you have at least one overcard, and you feel that a raise might provide an additional out or two. You essentially trade your flush odds for some extra outs. Calling is usually far better than raising with a draw in a multiway pot when the player to your right bets.

Playing small pairs after the flop

You hold a pair of sevens or less, and get to see a flop cheaply in five-way action. You miss your set on a board that features two overcards. What do you do after a bet and two calls?

I sure hope you said, "Fold," but even that is not enough. You also actually have to do it at the table. Calling in the hope of hitting your set on the turn is very seductive. After all, it is only one more small bet, there are several in there already (well, eight but who's counting?) and if you hit your set, you might win a big pot.

True, but the pot will not be big enough. A call is a 22-to-1 dog to hit a set. If you call, you must have a reasonable expectation of making more than 25 bets (as again, you might still lose). With eight bets in there now, you will need to win seventeen more, or 8½ big bets. Where will they come from? Let's say you do hit your set on the turn. There is a bet and call into you, you raise, and they both call. Now on the river, you bet and get a crying call. You will certainly win a nice-sized pot, but still not big enough to compensate for the 22 times you will miss and fold.

Players remember those rare seemingly large victories, but not the steady drip-drip-drip of one small bet going down the drain 22 times for each one they hit. Except in rare cases with a very large pot pre-flop, you should simply fold with a small pair when you miss a set. Yes, there will be times you will slap your forehead because your set comes on the turn after you fold, but you still show a nice profit by keeping your chips in your stack.

Conclusion

Most poker books, including this one, tell you about all of the plays and options you have available on the flop. I want to mention that often the best play is FOLD.

Going too far with a hand when you are not getting a good price, or when the hand you are trying to make may still not win, is one of the biggest leaks you can have. It also comes up often, so it compounds itself many times over the course of a session. Finally, you will win a few of these and not realize you have a major leak.

Think your way through the flop phase, planning your play, studying your opponents, optimizing your chances to win, and controlling pot size so you build pots when you are a likely winner. And let go when your chances are not worth the price.

Part Two: Stages

On the Turn

Chapter Eighteen

Turn Play Overview

The turn is arguably the most difficult street to play. Because the stakes are doubled, errors are magnified. If you happen to be betting or calling with the second best hand, you may call the river as well, thus making an even larger error. Many opponents, especially tougher ones, apply unrelenting pressure on the turn, making your decisions much more difficult.

Let's look at the situations you may find yourself in on the turn:

1. You believe you have the best hand.
2. You are drawing.
3. You have a good hand, but it may not be best.
4. You were bluffing on the flop.

1. You believe you have the best hand

Many times you have what seems to be the best hand. This can happen two ways.

♠ You started with the best hand and nothing bad seems to have happened.

♠ You made a draw.

You started with the best hand and nothing bad seems to have happened

Of course, there is almost always a possibility that you are beat, but you should generally assume that what appears to be the best hand probably is.

Example

You hold K♣-K♦, and the flop is J♥-8♠-3♥. You bet, and two people call. The turn is a 5♦. Sure you may be beat, but you must assume you are best. You will almost always bet or raise here.

In general, this situation also applies to top pair, top kicker situations.

You made a draw

If you make your draw in position, go ahead and bet or raise. If you make your draw out of position, you need to decide whether to bet out or check-raise. Base your decision on the following criteria:

♠ How strong a hand you made.

♠ The probability that someone will bet.

♠ Whether you can trap several players for extra bets.

♠ Balance – how you have played in this situation before.

If you are unsure of the correct strategy, bet. It is never terrible to get money into the pot when you think you have the best hand. This topic is covered in greater detail in Chapter 22 – Playing the Turn from out of Position.

2. You are drawing

In general, if you are drawing, count your outs and decide whether you are getting the right price to continue (including implied odds). If you are, call and hope to draw out; if not, fold to any bets.

Remember that there are "pure" outs and "impure" outs. Pure ones will win you the pot almost all or all the time. Impure outs are ones that will give you what you are drawing to, but may not win.

Worse are impure outs that, if you make one, will give you a hand that has to call on the end, but has a good chance of not winning.

Example

You have A-A and get raised on the turn by an opponent looking at a board of J♥-10♠-8♣-5♦. If he has a straight or a set, you are drawing dead. If he has two pair, you are live to an ace or either of the other two cards he does not hold pairing (if he holds J-10, you will win with an ace, eight, or five). However, if you do hit a pair, you will still not know if you have anything worthwhile, and it will usually cost you a bet to find out. The pot needs to give you a significant overlay before you can try for those outs, assuming you trust the raise that tells you that you are beat.

There are several other less frequent possibilities, based on how you played the flop:

- ♠ You raised for a free card.
- ♠ You bet the flop in position as a semi-bluff.
- ♠ You bet the flop out of position as a semi-bluff.
- ♠ You called on the flop, but may want to bet or raise the turn.

You raised for a free card

Assuming your plan worked, you have been checked to on the turn. You will often be tempted to bet here, but should resist the temptation. Only if you are heads-up should you consider betting, and then only against opponents who are aggressive enough to bet the flop, but cautious enough or fear you enough to fold the turn. This combination will rarely happen.

You bet the flop in position as a semi-bluff

Everyone checked to you on the flop, and you had a draw. You bet, hoping to win it right there, but your plan did not work.

Apply the same principle as you did with a free card raise: Check in a multiway pot, but usually bet against one opponent, unless he is a calling station. Many players take a card off on the flop, but almost routinely plan to fold the turn if they do not improve. Give your lone opponent a chance to do so. This play provides balance, as you will also continue to bet your made hands.

You bet the flop out of position as a semi-bluff

This is a close decision, and depends on many factors, as discussed in Chapter 22 – Playing the Turn from out of Position. As a general rule, if you are going to call anyway, you may as well bet and hope to win it. After all, you thought you had a chance to win it on the flop; maybe you will win it this time. If the turn card looks like it helped other players, or may be scary enough to get you a free card because everyone will check behind you, you can make an exception and check.

You called on the flop, but may want to bet or raise the turn

You did not act aggressively on the flop, and you have only a draw, but you should still consider aggressive action now. If the turn card could scare your opponent, think about how you would play the hand if it really did help you. Then play accordingly, betting, raising, or check-raising. Be aware that if you do not make your draw, you will have to carry out your deception on the river as well.

 TIP: Always consider playing a draw aggressively on the turn, even though you will usually call.

3. You have a good hand, but it may not be best

The most difficult hands to play are those you can't be sure about. You are either ahead or second best, and you cannot be sure which.

You will definitely make many mistakes in this situation. In our game of incomplete information, you will call people down and find out you were second best, and you will fold winners. Your objective is to strike a balance between seeing "monsters under the bed" and folding all the time, and being so optimistic that you turn into a calling station who never believes an opponent. Making the right plays here requires a combination of judgment, people reading, hand reading, and math.

Let's take a look at a few examples. There are several ways you may be unsure about your holding's relative strength. I will focus on only four of them:

♠ There are one or more overcards to your pair.

♠ A scare card comes.

♠ You have overcards like A-K or A-Q and do not know if your hand is best.

♠ You have top pair, less than top kicker, and it may not be best.

There are one or more overcards to your pair

One overcard in a small field (one or two opponents) is not that dangerous. Certainly, you must pay attention to the previous betting and the likely hands of the opponents, but you should continue to bet your hand until someone tells you (by raising) that your hand is not best. Then you need to decide if they are telling the truth.

More than one overcard, or a larger field, demands more respect. If both are present, fold when someone bets unless you have strong evidence that your hand may be good.

Let's go through an example to see just how complex turn play can be.

Example

A middle position player raises pre-flop. A late player calls, as does the small blind. You call in the big blind with J♠-10♣. The flop is 10♦-6♠-3♥. You bet out to observe the raiser's reaction. He calls, and the others fold.

First, let's do some hand reading. He raised pre-flop but did not raise your bet. What might that tell you?

First, it indicates he does not automatically raise on the flop when he raises pre-flop and someone bets into him. This is obvious on the face of it, but it is important information for later in the session. The flop has no reasonable draws for a pre-flop raiser (he is unlikely to hold 5-4), so he either has a pair or overcards.

If he has a pair, he would almost certainly raise to make sure the players behind him did not call with overcards that could beat him on the turn. Even if he holds say, 8-8, his correct play is to raise if he thinks you may have any pair or draw, and fold if he thinks you have a ten. Calling with only two possible outs if he is beat and two players to act behind him is a poor play. Yes, your opponents may make poor plays, but when reading hands, you should put decent players on reasonable plays. If he plays weakly, he will not be that readable but you will get his money sooner or later anyway.

So he either has overcards or pocket aces. With the latter, he could be willing to call the flop and raise on the turn to charge you double bets to continue, even though raising on the flop would have been a better play. He is much more likely to have some other overcards though, because there are so many combinations of them.

Now let's look at some different turn cards. Let's see how your play and thinking change if the turn card is

1.   Q♣
2.   Any other queen.
3.   5♥
4.   A♥

1. The turn is the Q♣

This card makes for a four-suited board, removing flush draws from the equation. Two of the overcard hands your opponent might hold have just gotten there (A-Q and K-Q). Or he could have an overpair to the board already and have slowplayed the flop, even though that is less likely due to the two players behind him (which is one of the reasons you bet into him).

Nevertheless, you must bet against all but the most aggressive and trickiest opponent. You are on solid ground if he calls or folds. If he raises, you can safely fold, since you do not have enough outs to continue.

If you are against one of those aggressive and tricky players, realize that if you bet, he may raise with A-K and A-J, representing a queen, especially if he thinks you have an underpair to the queen. In this case, checking and calling would be a better play. If you check to them on the turn, most of these players will bet regardless of their holding. This moves their bluffing frequency into the range where you can profitably call. You need not fear offering a free card to these players because they will never accept it, preferring to try to bully you instead.

2. The turn is any other queen

All of the other queens put a two-flush on the board. Let's assume it is the Q♥. This card emboldens some players with A♥-K♥ or A♥-J♥ to make a bluff raise, as they have picked up enough extra outs to justify it. As a result, you should bet, but you cannot honor a raise from a player capable of a semi-bluff raise quite as much as in the Q♣ case. Depending on the player, you may distrust him enough to play on. There will be times you will have to call all the way when an opponent suddenly gets frisky on the turn after a two-flush comes unless the flush completes or an ace or king comes.

3. The turn is the 5♥

This is not a scary turn card, but suppose you bet and get raised. Your opponent could have the pocket aces you fear, but could also have been influenced by getting a big flush draw. Call all but the most honest opponents down unless an ace hits on the river. Had the turn been the 5♣ (making a rainbow board), you could fold more often.

I want to remind you that this all depends on the read we made earlier that overpairs other than A-A were unlikely because of the two extra callers on the flop. If you were heads-up on the flop, your opponent's raise would be far more ominous, and folding would be correct more often.

4. The turn is the A♥

This card is very bad for you. Nearly all the hands he can have contain an ace. Only K-Q still survives as a hand you can beat. However, having seen an ace, you can figure this out by the numbers.

He can now have A-K and A-Q 12 ways each, and A-J nine ways (as you have a jack), for 33 cases that he has an ace. He will have K-Q 16 times. Assuming he is equally likely to have raised with any of these hands pre-flop, he is 33-16 to have an ace, or just about 2-to-1. The pot has five big bets (ignoring the small blind), so if you decide to check and call, you will have to put in two big bets to win seven. That is a possible plan, as it makes money assuming your opponent will bet every hand he holds to the river, ace or not. Some hyper-aggressive opponents will, but they are rare.

If you check the turn, he will always bet his ace to the river, but may take a free card with K-Q. Or he may bet K-Q once to see if you fold, but check it on the river and bet everything else. It would be nice to understand your opponent well enough to know which course of action he will take, but that is a lot to ask. He may even vary his actions. These facts make checking and calling a much less positive option. You may end up paying him every time he has an ace, but not getting paid when he does not.

How about betting? If you bet, he may not raise with an ace, as he will worry why you are not checking when the ace hits. In addition, all but the wildest or toughest opponents will not raise with K-Q (except perhaps K♥-Q♥ on occasion).

If you bet and he calls, you plan to check the river and decide whether to call. For that you will have to decide the odds that he would bluff with a K-Q. The fact is that most players will not bluff at the right frequency, so folding, even though the pot would have eight bets, would be a reasonable option. This is particularly true if you are known as a player who often calls, so your image counts here, too[7].

If you bet and he raises, you can now safely put him on an ace. But should you fold? With his raise, you are now getting 8-to-1. If he has A-K or A-Q, you have five outs. If he has A-J you have two. Even five outs is less than 8-to-1, and your implied odds are at most one bet. There is no overlay here, and you should fold.

It appears that betting will make you more money in the long run in this specific case than checking and calling will, unless your opponent will bet every hand, including K-Q, to the river. If that is the case, you are getting a price to call him down (you would win one-third of the time).

I spent extra time on this case to demonstrate how complex and delicate turn decisions can be. This was not a very complicated hand, as you were heads-up after the flop. It also demonstrates that it often pays to bet the turn even if what appears to be the worst-case overcard comes, as long as there are other hands your opponent may hold.

A scare card comes

Often, you dislike that turn card, as you did in the last example when the A♥ came on the turn. It may complete a possible flush or a possible straight, or it may just be an overcard. Since it didn't help you, the questions are:

♠ Did it help someone else?

♠ If so, how much?

---

[7] I know I am now talking about the river and this is a turn chapter. As I will discuss in Chapter 19, you cannot effectively deal with the turn unless you consider how you will play the river.

In aggressive games many players will use a scare card to represent a made hand, even if it just improved their drawing chances.

Example 1

A player with 8♦-7♦ calls a flop of Q♦-6♣-5♥. If a 7♠ hits the turn, this player may represent a made straight or two pair, even though he now has just a small pair and a straight draw. Of course, if he is against only one player, that small pair may be good. An opponent with J-J will have a difficult decision against such a player.

Example 2

Similarly, a player with K♠-Q♣ may play a flop of J♠-9♠-6♦ with a gutshot straight, two overcards, and a backdoor flush draw. Now if the 5♠ hits, he may decide to represent the flush, still holding many outs if no one else has already made a flush.

If this player is out of position, he may have check-called the flop. Now he suddenly bets on the turn, trying to take it down or to improve if called. Players like this figure it is almost impossible for an opponent holding a hand as good as aces (with no spade) to raise here, and equally tough for a player holding, say, A♥-K♥ to even stay around. However, if you are the player being bet into, stop and think. Many of these bettors do not have balance in their game. If they really made their hand, they would almost always try for a check-raise. For these players, leading here is almost like waving a red flag saying, "I'm semi-bluffing here."

Raise these players to make them pay the maximum for their draw. Very few of them will make a three-bet semi-bluff in response, so they call and hope to draw out. Even then, if they make it, they may try for a check-raise on the river (after all, you did raise the turn, so they certainly expect you to bet again), so checking behind them saves a bet when they draw out, and charges them the maximum when they don't. You will sometimes be wrong, but that's always true in poker. Call or fold to straightforward players while raising aggressive, check-raising ones in this situation.

What if you are in position in a multiway pot, believe you had the best hand on the flop, the scare card hits, and everyone checks? This is a tough situation, since you do not want to give a free card, but you also don't want to get check-raised. If you check, you can see the river for one bet at most (you will likely have to call the last bet because you induced a river bluff with your check), while if you bet and get raised, you may have to fold rather than see the river at all.

Let's address the free card first. Many players simply have a mantra, "No free cards." They bet all the time in this situation. However, giving free cards is not terrible if the opponent was going to call anyway. It costs you a fraction of a bet, which admittedly adds up over the long term, but that is not as significant a loss as incorrectly calling or folding to a check-raise.

If your bet is likely to get opponents to fold, go ahead and make it. If betting may cause you to fold to a check-raise, you need to assess the probability that they will fold, call, or check-raise, considering the following:

- ♠ How many players are there? (The fewer opponents, the less likely the scare card helped them.)
- ♠ Based on their earlier betting, what is the probability that the card actually helped someone?
- ♠ Can you improve to beat the hand they may have made? (The more chances to improve, the more likely you should check, as you do not want to fold to a check-raise.)
- ♠ Would these opponents have checked if they made the hand the scare card represents?
- ♠ Could the opponents think that the scare card helped you?

This last is a key question many players forget to ask. Scare cards work in two directions. Unless it helped one of your opponents, they have to worry that it may have helped you. This makes it harder for all but the most aggressive players to check-raise you with a semi-bluff unless they have good read on your hand already. You always want to think about what your opponents think you have, and that concept may be especially important here.

You have overcards like A-K or A-Q and do not know if your hand is best

You have A♦-K♣ and raise two limpers. Everyone else folds, and they call. The flop comes 10♣-9♣-6♥. On the flop, they check, you bet, and they call. The turn is the 3♠. They both check. They could easily be on draws here, like K-J, so you could have the best hand. Many players would automatically bet here, hoping either that they hold the best hand, can get a better hand (like 4-4) to fold, or might draw out.

I prefer to check. Most draws will keep playing anyway, so you are only losing a fraction of a bet by checking. Most made hands will put you on A-K and call you down. You can still draw out if an ace or king hits, and you cannot be check-raised out of the pot. You may even get a free showdown as well. You do need to bet occasionally to vary your play, but checking should be your default action.

If there was only one caller after you bet the flop, you could either:

- ♠ Bet the turn, hoping to improve or get checked to on the river, or
- ♠ Check the turn, planning to call the river regardless of what comes since you have induced a bluff.

Your decision depends on how you think the caller plays – the more passively he plays, the safer it is for you to bet the turn, as you are unlikely to get check-raised.

If there were three callers after the flop, you may have been better off not betting at all. Assuming you did bet the flop, if at least two of them are still there on the turn, checking is the best plan, even though there are still chances your hand is good.

You have top pair, less than top kicker, and it may not be best

If you are heads-up in position, use the way ahead or way behind principle (as described in Chapter 21). If you are heads-up out of position, bet the turn and fold to a raise, unless your opponent is wild or a frequent bluffer.

Multiway, you bet if there are any draws present, as you cannot resolve the ambiguous situation by checking, and you cannot afford to give free cards to the drawing players, especially if some of them may fold.

You were bluffing on the flop

As a general rule, if you bluffed the flop, you should bluff the turn as long as only one person is still in. Here, for example, is an *Illusion of Action* play.

Example

You hold 10♠-8♠ in the cutoff. Everyone folds to a loose raiser on your immediate right, who raises. You decide to make an *Illusion of Action* three-bet trying to take the play away from him, get the other players to fold, and create dead blind money. This works, and the raiser is the only caller. The flop hits J♦-6♣-2♣. Not your favorite, but he checks, you bet per plan, and he calls. Now the turn is a 3♥, and he checks again. Should you give up here, or spend more money on your weak hand?

Spend the money. Your bet here could easily win the pot. If he has a hand like K-Q, he may take one off on the flop, but he cannot call the turn. He may have taken one off with A♣-9♥ because of the overcard and backdoor flush draw. When you three-bet pre-flop, you pretty much committed yourself to at least following through on the turn unless something very bad happened. What actually happened wasn't all that good, but not terrible either. Remember that you made your *Illusion of Action* raise because of your tight image. Now is the time to try to use that image to win a pot.

Some players call bluffing in this manner, "riding the tiger". Once you are on a tiger, riding him to exhaustion is a heck of a lot better than jumping off.

Conclusion

Turn play is sufficiently complex that you should take any "rules" of play with a huge lump of salt. Here are some anyway:

♠ When you have taken the lead, generally keep the lead until someone tells you to stop.

♠ If you are drawing, consider bluffing against one opponent who may be weak. You will usually decide not to do it, but you should always keep it in mind.

♠ When you are drawing, remember there is a huge difference between cards that complete your hand but may still lose ("impure outs") and cards that will win the pot. Discount impure outs considerably. Also discount "outs" that will cost you a bet on the end if you make them and are wrong.

Chapter Nineteen

Other Turn Topics

It is almost impossible to deal with all of the possibilities that may happen on the turn. The topics below come up often enough to deserve special consideration.

- ♠ Planning your river play.
- ♠ Considering the impact of the turn card.
- ♠ Making tough turn decisions.

Planning your river play on the turn

One of the most important concepts is planning the turn and river together. Before making a play on the turn, think about how you will play the river.

Example

Say you have A♣-J♣ on the button, a middle position player raises, gets two cold callers and you call as well. The big blind also calls. The flop is A♦-8♣-6♠. After the big blind checks, the raiser bets, and one player calls. You call as well, and the blind folds. The turn card is the 3♣, giving you a flush draw. The raiser bets again, and the other player folds. You should raise, not because you are certain you have the best hand, but because you are certainly going to call a river bet. If your opponent folds, that's great because you win. If he calls, you plan to check the river behind him unless that card is a club or a jack, in which case you will bet. There is a slim chance he will reraise, but it is quite small, since he cannot know that you do not have a set or two pair.

Much of what you do on the turn is influenced by your river plan. If, as above, you call the turn and plan to call the river, at least consider the impact of raising. If you are in position and everyone checks to you, your decision to bet or check must take into account your plan for dealing with raises on this street and how you wish to play the river. If you are heads-up out of position and deciding whether to semi-bluff the turn, you must also decide before betting whether you will follow through on the river if you miss. Not only may your conclusion affect whether or not you bet, but it will help eliminate hesitation tells when you do bet the river.

Considering the impact of the turn card

Determining your continuation concept on the turn depends on your flop plan, and how the turn card affected it. Let's look at a simple example.

Example

You held 9♠-8♠, and called on the button after three limpers. Both blinds called. The flop was K♦-7♠-5♣. The small blind bet, and two players called. With 10 small bets in the pot, you had to call only one. Holding a gutshot for a nut straight (four outs) and a backdoor flush (roughly one out) you had an easy call, especially as you were last to act and could not be raised. The turn was the 2♦. The small blind bet again, and one person called to you. You original plan was to take one off with the right odds and see if you made your gutshot, or a second spade fell, allowing you to continue. Neither happened. Now the pot holds seven big bets so you are not close to getting the right price to continue. You fold.

Let's look at how you would have played other turn cards:

♠ A six. Of course, you would have raised.

♠ A spade. You would call with 12 likely outs. A semi-bluff raise would risk a three-bet and terrible odds. It would also have little chance to work against two players, but it was good that you thought about it. Always consider all possible plays before selecting one.

♠ The 9♦. You would have to reassess your chances of winning. You would have a pair and a gutshot, but a possible flush draw would be present. A non-diamond six would give you a one-card straight that would almost certainly be good, though it could be for only half the pot. A river eight would give you two pair, but any eight could give someone a straight, and the 8♦ may give someone a backdoor flush. Assessing your outs, you would have three clean sixes, one compromised six, two nines, and three compromised eights. You would have somewhere near seven total outs, none of which give you the nuts, and your straight could possibly be chopped. I put this at about five to six effective outs. Calling it 5.5, give you roughly one chance out of 7.5, not good enough for the 7-to-1 pot odds. You may make another bet or two if you win, but you may just as easily lose another bet if you make your hand and lose, so implied odds are not significant. You should take the conservative approach and fold.

So much for the "simple" example, which got pretty complex if certain cards hit. This is the dilemma of the turn. That one card forces you to reassess your plan and perhaps form an entirely new one.

Making tough turn decisions

Some of the toughest decisions in poker happen on the turn. Most of your tough turn decisions that do not involve scare cards happen when you have made it to the turn with moderate values and do not know whether you are ahead or behind. In one typical scenario, you raised or reraised pre-flop and bet the flop. Now you have seen the turn card, but still don't have very much.

If you are still in a multiway pot, you should almost always give up, particularly if you are out of position. Of course, your decision still depends on the size of the pot, the texture of the board, your chances of improving and the nature of your opponents. Let's look at some examples.

Example 1

You open-raise in late middle position with A♣-10♣, and the button and big blind call. The flop is K♦-6♠-2♣, giving you nothing. After the big blind checks, you bet and both opponents call. The turn is the 9♠, and the big blind checks. You should check and fold to a bet. You have nothing, there are no draws, and the pot contains only five big bets. Even if your opponents call flops liberally, one of them rates to have you beat, and you have few if any outs. It is time to give up. OK, that was not such a tough decision, even though many players would bet here again. Let's look at the same situation with a different flop and turn.

Suppose instead the flop is 8♠-8♦-3♣. Again both players call your bet on the flop. If the turn is the 5♥, bet again. You could easily have the best hand, as either opponent could have overcards to the board that do not beat yours.

 TIP: As a general rule, if you can plausibly hold the best hand with overcards against one or two opponents, bet the turn. If there are more players in, giving up would be the best play.

Example 2

Same situation, but now the flop is Q♦-J♦-8♣. Same two players call. The turn is the 5♥. This is a tougher decision, since you have some outs if you are behind, but you may equally be ahead against hands like K-10, K-9, A-9, and A♦-3♦, or even 10-7, all of which would call the flop, but some may fold if you bet the turn. If you had only one opponent, you would continue to bet, but with this many cards in the playing zone (ace through nine) and two opponents, one of them probably has at least a pair and probably will not let it go. Check here and see what the button does.

If it goes bet-raise, you have an easy fold. If the button bets and the big blind calls, you will be getting around 6.5-to-1 to call. You have three outs to the nuts (kings), one other king which will be good if no one holds diamonds, four nines to make a straight, which may win, lose, or chop, and possible outs if you hit your ace. This is at least six effective outs and possibly seven, but still not enough to justify a call. You can count at least one bet in implied odds if you hit a non-diamond king, but you may still lose extra bets on the river if you catch an ace or nine and it is no good. Admittedly this is a close call with a double gutshot and an overcard, but the smallish pot and presence of suited cards tilts the difference towards folding.

Interestingly, if the button bets and the big blind folds, your situation changes. Now your pot odds are worse, but the chances you can win unimproved go way up, especially if the button would bet his draws here. While you are only getting a little better than 5.5-to-1 to hit your draws, you must consider the chances that you have the best hand and will win a showdown. Also, if you spike a non-diamond nine against only one opponent, the chances improve that you will win or tie (in fact, you can lose only if you are way ahead right now because that means he has K-10). Your ace outs go up in value as well. Here your decision comes down to how you think the button plays. If he is timid and will almost always bet his real hands and check his draws, you have to fold. If he will automatically bet if you check to him, then you have to at least call, and a check-raise semi-bluff might win the pot for you right here if he would fold a hand like 7-7 (which he would play hoping you had A-K). This is a guessing game, and you will be wrong some of the time no matter what you do, but that is the nature of tough turn decisions. Just make the best choice you can and live with the consequences.

Many of the toughest decisions come when you either hold A-K and missed the flop and turn, or have made an *Illusion of Action* play. Let's look at both of these.

Playing A-K

This discussion assumes you have missed the flop and turn, so you have no pair. Rather than pick a sample hand or two for the A-K case, let's develop general rules for continuation. Here are the topics we will cover:

1. Number of opponents.
2. How the opponents play.
3. Presence of draws on the board.
4. Presence of calling zone cards on the board.
5. Your drawing prospects.

1. Number of opponents

As is usually the case, the more opponents you have, the more likely one of them already has you beat. If you are beat on the turn, you would certainly prefer not to bet, as your chances to improve are limited and making an ace or king on the river is never a sure out. All other things being equal, bet vs. one opponent, check against three or more, and use other criteria to determine whether to bet against two. However, the other criteria also matter, and may combine to outweigh this general rule.

There is one more case where the number of opponents matters. Occasionally, someone will raise before the flop after several limpers with A-K, and have four or five opponents. They all check to him, and he checks. Now the turn comes and does not seem threatening. All of the opponents check again. With what I consider astonishing frequency, the A-K player now bets. He seems to assume that if all of these guys checked twice, his A-K must be good and he would err by giving up another free card. The chances that all of the players have no pair are less than the 5-to-1 the pot is offering the A-K player. Plus, the chances of a check-raise are high, as many tough players check the turn expecting the optimistic bet from the pre-flop raiser.

Do not make this error. With that many opponents, just assume you are behind, even though you may be wrong on occasion. Take the extra free card rather than hope that everyone has nothing and will fold.

2. How the opponents play

As in all poker decisions, it helps to understand how your opponents play, and sometimes even how they play specifically against you. Would they have bet out with a pair or better to keep you from checking and taking a free card? Would they have check-raised the flop with a pair or better? Are they likely to put you on specifically A-K and check-raise the turn with any hand that can beat you? Every opponent and situation is unique, and making this assessment and the consequent decision to check or bet with your A-K improves as your ability to react effectively to your opponents increases. Against passive opponents, especially those who will let you win a free showdown with an unimproved ace, bet the turn liberally. Bet also against opponents who typically will bet into you on the flop with a decent hand. Tend to check against tricky or aggressive opponents who like to check-raise.

3. Presence of draws on the board

Dead boards are dangerous. The more draws that are present on the board, the more likely your opponent does not hold a made hand, and thus you should bet what could easily still be best hand.

Example

If your opponent checks and calls on a Q♥-7♣-3♠ flop, the chances are he either has a pair or is one of those guys that calls every flop. Assuming you know it is not the latter, you are generally behind. If the board is 10♠-9♠-6♦, your opponents' check-call may be based on any number of draws including gutshots like A-8 and K-J. Be more likely to bet into these boards.

4. Presence of calling zone cards on the board

The worst cards to see on the flop are queens and jacks. First, many opponents either limp or love to call with hands containing these cards. Second, they do not have overcards to justify their call on the flop. Third, the presence of these cards taints your outs, in that A-Q, A-J, K-Q, and K-J are hands many like to play for your raise, and your outs are cut in half if they hold a pair with one of these hands. On the other hand, against typical middle-limit opponents, cards nine or lower are much safer for you, as your opponents can have overcards to call the flop and you will still be in the lead. Be extra wary of betting into boards with queens and jacks on them, especially if they came on the flop.

5. Your drawing prospects

Many boards offer extra outs to A-K, either in the form of a flush draw or an inside straight draw. Some players believe the presence of these draws gives them a better turn bet, as they may win by their opponents folding or by drawing out. This is a fine idea if you are fairly sure you will not be check-raised, but if you are, you will either have to lay down your hand because you are getting the wrong price, or call the raise and pay two big bets for what you could have seen for nothing. Your judgment of whether your opponent is more likely to fold, call, or check-raise will determine your action, but when in doubt, with draws take the free card. However, if you check the turn, be prepared to call a bet on the river as you have induced a bluff, and you do not have to be right very often to call profitably here.

Take all of these factors into account in determining how to proceed with an unimproved A-K on the turn.

After an *Illusion of Action* play

Here we are discussing a play in which you three-bet before the flop with a marginal hand to get heads-up in position with an opponent and kill the blinds. Assuming you were successful in this, you bet the flop and were called. You still have nothing and have to decide how to continue on the turn.

In general, bet. You knew you were bluffing when you started this, and successful bluffing requires commitment and follow-through. However, if an ace hits the board, either on the flop or on the turn, slow down. Many opponents will call the flop with A-K or A-Q planning to fold the turn if they do not improve. Betting the turn will get them to give you the pot unless they pick up a draw, are unduly suspicious (in which case your *Illusion of Action* play was poorly timed), or are simply stubborn. Aces are your enemy here even if you have one, as you can easily be out-kicked. The best you can do is check the turn, call the river bet, and see who wins.

Conclusion

Turn play, though quite complex, is easier if you always think in terms of your plan. You made a plan on the flop, and saw what happened.

Assess the meaning of your opponents' actions, consider the impact of the turn card, and revise your plan. Take into account how you wish to play the river (assuming you plan to get there). Then take decisive action, whether that is leading out, checking and folding, or raising in the hopes of either winning or getting a free showdown.

Chapter Twenty

Raising the Turn

Like a phone call from the IRS, an opponent's raise on the turn can be quite intimidating. Because of this, many players raise the turn with a variety of different hand types, particularly when in position. In some games, this raise means, "I have you beat, and you are in trouble." But in middle- and higher-limit games, sophisticated competitors use the heads-up turn raise in position to mean an abundance of things. Let's look at the ways you can use this bet.

You have a big hand

Yes, annoyingly enough, one of the main uses of raising the turn still means what it always did. In fact, it is the threat of this possibility that makes the play so powerful and makes the other meanings difficult to deal with.

You are going to call the river and might improve

Usually, players raise here with some chances to improve.

Example

You have A♠-Q♦ and three-bet a middle position raiser. Everyone folds, and you take the flop heads-up. The flop

comes A♣-J♠-6♠ and your opponent bets. He may well
have you beat here with A-K or A-J, or he could be betting
a pair of kings or queens, or a weaker ace. While raising
the flop seems attractive, a reraise would be unwelcome,
and you would like to see the hand develop. After the turn
card comes 8♠, your opponent bets again. Now a raise will
be very effective, as he cannot know that you do not
already have a flush. He might fold a better hand, which
would be great, or a weaker hand that still has outs. If he
does call, he will almost certainly check the river, in which
case you will also check unless you have picked up a flush
and can bet again. Also, the raise can make you an extra
bet when the spade does come. If you just call the turn, he
will certainly check a spade on the river and you will
collect, at best, two big bets instead of three.

You are going to call the river

Even if you do not feel you have a lot of outs, a raise on the turn still
might be effective against many opponents who are fairly passive or
timid. Whenever you are sure you are going to call your opponent on the
river, you should consider raising. After all, your opponent might figure
you for a more powerful hand and release. If not, you check the river
behind him and see who wins. However, there are two downsides to this
play. First, if your opponent has an excellent hand, he might reraise, and
you will likely be forced to fold. Second, if your opponent is really
passive, he might decide to check the river even if you did not raise, and
you could have seen the showdown for one bet instead of the two it
would cost you to raise. You need to be careful here when you believe
you have few or no possible additional outs.

You have a semi-bluff

Another popular meaning for this raise is a semi-bluff, which is a hand
which cannot be best right now, but might improve to the best hand or
will win when the opponent folds. When this play works, it is very
gratifying because you either win right now, or you show down a hand
you made on the river, and get credit (or ridicule) for "raising on the
come", thus enhancing your image as a gambler. This usage was more
effective before the raise became so popular, because it is getting tougher

to get people to lay down their hand to a raise on the turn. In addition, you are faced with the dilemma of what to do when you miss your draw and are checked to on the river. There is a lot to be said for betting as a bluff, of course, since it is now the only way to win the pot, and the pot has grown large. But this makes your overall play cost three big bets, when it might have only cost one (calling the turn and folding when you do not improve). You really need to consider both pot size and your opponent's tendencies before trying a play like this.

You are bluffing

Of course, you can simply bluff raise. While this seems to have all of the problems of a semi-bluff raise without the offset of being able to make your hand, this play can be an effective defence against aggressive players who frequently bet with nothing.

For example, assume you are in the big blind and everyone folds to the small blind. You are facing a very aggressive small blind, who raises. You call, and the flop does not help you. Of course, giving up is certainly an excellent option, but missing happens frequently. You cannot give up every time, especially when you have position. If you chose to continue, calling the flop planning to bluff raise the turn no matter what card hits is a fine variety play, and plays into the *Illusion of Action*. Sure, it will be expensive when your opponent actually has a strong hand, but he will miss the flop as often as you do. Also, since you have a tight image, your raise will be scary even if he does have a little bit of the board. I am not recommending you use this bluff-raise-on-the-turn-in-position very often, but occasions do arise when it has good chances.

Using these plays

Notice that the above list of hand types covers virtually all of the hands you might hold when you are in position on the turn. Should you always raise?

No, of course not. The power of the play depends on its credibility, which means you should usually have a big hand, just like the bet says. This is especially true if your turn raises are getting called, which is also happening more frequently in games where the "could mean anything" turn raise is prevalent.

Most of your other turn raises should be of the "I am going to call anyway, and I might improve" flavor. The others are very risky, and you should rarely use them. Even as *Illusion of Action* plays, they do not have much to recommend them. To capitalize on the loose turn-raising image, you will need to pick up a series of excellent hands and get bet into, and this is hard to do. And, as we noted before, skeptical opponents may call you anyway. In general, if you do not have very much, do not look for chances to put in extra big bets.

Some of your opponents will make these plays, so you do need to be aware of them. In fact, in some games you will find your opponents positively addicted to them. At a minimum, you need to make fewer laydowns against these players, and (at least) call them down more often than you otherwise might.

Chapter Twenty-One

Way Ahead or Way Behind

On almost every hand, someone has the lead, and all of the other players are striving to outdraw him. So someone is always ahead, and everyone else is behind. But a special category of situations termed "Way Ahead or Way Behind" has particular characteristics, and you need to play hands in this category in a specific manner. This chapter defines the term, gives a brief standard example, and looks at a hand in which many of the principles come into play.

A "Way Ahead or Way Behind" situation requires the following:

- ♠ You are heads-up.
- ♠ You do not know whether you are ahead or behind.
- ♠ If you are ahead, your opponent very few outs (typically two or three).
- ♠ If you are behind, you have very few outs.

These situations come up in a lot of ways, but most frequently when you have an ace with a decent kicker.

Example

A typical scenario: you have A♥-J♦ and three-bet a loose middle position raiser from the button. The big blind and the raiser call. The flop comes A♠-6♣-2♦, you bet, the big blind folds, and your opponent calls. The turn is the 5♥ and your opponent checks. If he has A-K or A-Q, you are way behind and must catch a jack to win. However, if he has a pocket pair or a weaker ace, he has three or fewer outs unless he has hit his kicker already, in which case you have exactly as many outs as if he had A-K or A-Q.

It would be nice to bet here, planning to check the river, but if he has A-K (and possibly A-Q) he will check-raise, and you will have to fold, not getting the right price to hit your three-out hand. If he has a pair, he may fold and you will collect the pot, but no extra bets.

If he will call you down with most big pairs, bet and risk the check-raise. If he will fold many hands weaker than yours, then checking behind him and playing for a one-bet ending is a better strategy. With a better hand than yours, he will bet the river, and you will lose only one more bet. You also get to see the river for free with a chance to draw out.

With a worse hand than yours, he may still bet the river as a (misguided) value bet[8], or check and call your river bet, believing you may be trying to buy the pot. These additional bets add up over time.

Frequently, these situations are tricky for both players since neither may know whether he is leading or trailing. Sometimes your opponent will be the aggressor and represent that he is way ahead, but you cannot be certain enough to fold.

Let's look at a slightly more complex situation.

Example

You are in the cut-off with K♣-Q♣ and, after everyone folds in front of you, you raise. The button folds, and the

---

[8] See Chapter 23 for a discussion of value betting.

small blind reraises. This knocks out the big blind, making you heads-up.

The small blind is a tough player, and you take a moment to decide what sort of hand he can have here. Because you raised in late position, he does not have to give you credit for a premium hand, so his raise will have a wider range than if you had raised from early position. Also, because he is in the small blind, his raise has a chance to knock out the big blind, which is another reason he might have a less than premium hand. Of course, he would also raise with excellent hands as well.

You elect to call the raise, since folding is out of the question, and reraising is speculative as your hand could easily be second best to any ace or any pocket pair. The flop provides some help for you: K♥-8♦-3♠. Your opponent bets out. What should you do now?

You realize that you really have no idea where you stand. If he has A-A, A-K, or K-K, you are far behind with five, three, and zero outs respectively. On the other hand, if he has a hand like pocket queens, jacks, or tens, then *he* has two outs. If he has A-Q or A-J, again he has three outs. If his hand is somehow worse than ace-high or a pair, he is drawing nearly dead.

If you raise here, he will probably fold a worse hand and reraise with a better one. But, being a tough player, he might occasionally reraise with a hand you could beat as a way of testing your hand (since you might raise as a bluff yourself) or testing your resolve.

The real key here is that if he is behind, you want to keep him in, preferably having him bet, as he has very few ways to win, and he can have many more hands that are behind than ahead. In fact, a call by you might even convince him he should bluff at the turn with nothing at all hoping (forlornly) that you will fold. So, while raising is not a bad play, calling has many more advantages here.

After you call his flop bet, the turn is the 6♣, and your opponent now checks. Again, take a moment and decide what you would do.

Many people would say to bet here, since they would not want to give a free card that might beat them even if the opponent has only a couple of outs. Let's look at this situation in more depth, though.

Analyzing the turn play

Because he is a good player, he realizes that you have some sort of hand yourself. If you had nothing, you would have folded on the flop. Therefore, if he is way ahead, this would be a terrific time for him to check-raise. So if he is ahead, you certainly want to check, not bet.

But what if you are ahead? Almost certainly, a bet by you will win the pot, while a check will risk losing it. Interestingly, though, there is another factor to consider. If you do check here, how will your opponent act on the river?

By creating doubt in his mind about your hand here, you may very well get him to call you on the river (or even bluff the river if he does not improve). For example, if he has pocket fives, he probably would fold here if you bet, not wanting to call both the turn and river. If you check the turn, you will lose when he hits his two-outer, but might gain a bet when he does not.

Let's look at the math in the pocket jacks case. After your call on the flop, the pot holds nine small bets. If you bet now, you will win the nine bets almost all the time. Of course, if he calls with his losing hand so much the better, but you can't count on it. If you check, one time in 23 he will hit his set and bet. You will call and lose an additional big bet. However, 22 of 23 times he will miss. In those cases, he will either bet or check and call most of the time. You will win two extra small bets 22 times, and lose 11 small bets once in every 23 plays.

Remarkably, you profit hugely in this case by checking and giving him a chance to catch up. Yes, when he does catch up, you lose a pot you might have won, but when he does not, he almost certainly loses a big bet he would not have lost otherwise.

The rewards greatly outweigh the risks because:

- ♠ The pot is fairly small,
- ♠ He rarely catches up, and
- ♠ The number of extra calls you might get is relatively large.

So on this hand, if he is way ahead, you certainly want to check, and if he is way behind, you also want to check! Clearly you cannot do all of this math and figuring at the table after he checks, but by studying and recognizing this repeating theme, you should be able to make the correct play based on your general knowledge.

The river becomes very easy after that. You want to play for a one-bet scenario. If he bets, you call; if he checks, you bet. This type of "Way Ahead or Way Behind" situation gets resolved in this manner.

Conclusion

While "Way Ahead or Way Behind" confrontations are somewhat common, you must be careful to identify them correctly. If your opponent is semi-bluffing, for example, with eight or nine or more outs, then you must play far more aggressively. Only when you can be sure you are in a textbook "Way Ahead or Way Behind" situation can you afford the passive play that typically optimizes your results.

Recognizing these situations and reacting to them properly takes time and study. Once you understand the principles, however, you should be using these situations to lose less when you are way behind, and show a larger profit when you are way ahead.

Chapter Twenty-Two

Playing the Turn from out of Position

Most texts offer only generalities about playing the turn, and I don't blame them. So much happens pre-flop and on the flop that comprehensive discussions of turn play become very complex.

But we can discuss a small segment of turn play with some thoroughness. This chapter will review situations in which you are first to act on the turn. I have selected this topic for several reasons:

- ♠ Playing in position is easier. You can check, bet, or raise with a much clearer picture of what is happening.
- ♠ I recommend avoiding being out of position, but there are times when we can't avoid it.
- ♠ Too many players defer automatically to the in-position opponents, simply checking and calling (or folding).

We will consider the following situations:

- ♠ You checked the flop, and you called.
- ♠ You checked the flop, and you raised.
- ♠ You checked the flop, and no one bet.

♠ You bet the flop, and no one raised.

♠ You bet the flop, got raised, and you called.

♠ You bet the flop, got raised, and you reraised.

For all of these cases, we will look at most of the possible reasons you should or should not bet on the turn.

You checked the flop, and you called

This may be the most interesting situation, and it comes up first. If you checked the flop and simply called, why would you now consider betting? There are four reasons:

1. You were slowplaying your hand.
2. You have just made your hand.
3. You have just picked up a big draw.
4. You think the turn card did not help the opponent, and you wish to bluff.

Let's examine each of them and see which ones you should bet and when.

1. You were slowplaying your hand

The primary reasons for checking and calling with a made hand on the flop are deception or fear that a bet will eliminate players.

For example, you have a tight image and after you get a free play in the blind, you flop a surprising two pair. The flop is non-threatening, and you think that a bet will cause the other players to fold. You check against, say, three players, and the last one bets. Again, you don't want to check-raise because you want the others to call as well. Two of them do. Now the turn makes a possible draw. You do not want to give the field a free card, and you think that there is an excellent chance that the player who bet will check here. In this case you should certainly bet.

However, if the player who bet is aggressive and frequently auto-bets the turn, or if the turn card looks like it might have hit him, you might be better off check-raising to make sure you get an additional bet or two.

If you are heads-up on the turn, you will want to balance your play here, sometimes betting, even into a frequent bettor, and sometimes check-raising.

Of course, your hand may be stronger than two pair. Perhaps you flopped the nut straight or even a full house. Your decision to check the flop would depend on how many players there were, and how likely they would be to call. Once you checked and called, your decision becomes similar.

You should bet if there are draws present to make sure that you get your opponents to put money in before they miss and fold for free. In fact, failure to bet here, trying to be clever with a flopped full house or quads, is a common error. Having someone else bet your big hand for you twice can be fun, but unless you are nearly certain this will happen, you need to do your own work.

2. You have just made your hand

Many players check almost without thinking when they should bet, thinking, "I checked and called. Now I can check-raise."

That would be unsophisticated thinking. When you make you hand on the turn and are first to act, you should consider several things. First, how obvious is your made hand? A flush card hitting on the turn is pretty clear to everyone, and thus the bettor is more likely to check. If an overcard hits you, especially if you represented overcards before the flop, it probably pays to just bet out.

Perhaps you hit trips, generally when you called with middle pair. Again, betting against most opponents would be your best choice. Unsophisticated opponents will not believe you because with trips they would have tried to check-raise. Sophisticated players may read hands well enough to check the turn behind you. Even against hyper-aggressive opponents, who would always bet if you checked, you should consider betting because they might be skeptical or brazen enough to raise.

If you make a well-hidden straight, you have a better chance that someone else will bet, and you can consider checking, but only if you can trap several unsuspecting opponents for an extra bet. Even then, sometimes betting can win you more money, as check-raising may alert them to the fact you have a monster, while they may think you are betting out for many reasons.

One reason to bet out is to establish that you do so when you make your hand. At first, people will be skeptical and call you down. This is fine because it means your good hands are getting paid off. But eventually some observant opponents will realize that you have what you say you have on the turn and start folding to your bets.

While it may seem that you are now losing bets, this actually creates opportunities to bluff on the turn when a scare card hits. Now, since these opponents "know" that you have what you're representing, you can pick up whole pots by simply betting occasionally.

3. You have just picked up a big draw

This is a fairly common reason to bet, especially against only one or two opponents. And it does not work as well as most practitioners expect.

For example, you check and call with straight draw. Now the turn card gives you a flush draw as well. Should you think, "Wow, now I have a lot of outs. I may as well semi-bluff and perhaps win right here"?

Unfortunately, you also need to decide exactly what your bet represents. If the board is otherwise non-threatening, you are probably trying to represent that you just made two pair. But if you did hit a well-hidden two pair, wouldn't you be more likely to check-raise? Most players would. So your bet has very little credibility, and many aggressive players will tend to raise you on general principles when you make this bet, particularly if they have an overpair.

Now you have the dilemma of calling and demonstrating that you had a big draw, or risking even more money with a brave three-bet that still has only a small chance to succeed.

The straightforward play would be to check and call, and there is no shame in playing that way most of the time. An alternative would be a bluff check-raise, which would be consistent with the hidden two-pair play. Before trying this expensive play, be sure that your opponent can lay down a hand when he feels he is beat.

4. You think the turn card did not help your opponent, and you wish to bluff

This case is closely related to the last one in that you will be bluffing. The difference is that you have not improved, and your best chance to win is to bet and hope your opponent folds. I say "opponent" because if there is more than one you should very rarely try a naked bluff.

Of course, this is still probably a semi-bluff because you would not have called the flop bet with nothing at all. But it is probably a hand that will have to fold if you check and he bets.

For this play to work, not only does the turn card have to miss your opponent, but it also has to make a possible hand for you to represent. Some players think that a third flush card would work here, but unless you have a lot of credibility, your opponent could easily put you on a flush draw, perhaps with a pair.

Example

The most typical situation for this would be a four-straight or four-flush on the board, with the straight being the most common because you are better able to judge that your opponent would not have been helped. For example, you call a pre-flop raise in the big blind with J♣-10♣. The flop is 4♣-5♥-7♣. You check and call. The turn is the 6♠, which almost certainly does not help your opponent. It doesn't help you either, but it could have. So a bet here forces your opponent, even with a big pair, to realize he will have to call two more big bets while possibly drawing dead. He could easily give up.

You checked the flop, and you raised

At first glance, this seems like a no-brainer. You check-raised, and now it's your turn again. Surely you will just bet.

Most of the time you will, but there are a few cases when you may want to check instead:

1. You were semi-bluffing and missed.
2. You raised for value with a draw and missed.
3. You were semi-bluffing or raising for value, and hit.
4. Your big hand became bigger.
5. You thought you had the best hand, but the turn was bad for you.

6. Nothing happened, and you think you still have the best hand.

1. You were semi-bluffing and missed

Typically, this happens when you become heads-up after the flop. Say a late position player raises, and you call in the big blind with 10♣-8♣ after the small blind calls. The flop is A♥-9♠-7♣, so you are open ended. You both check to the raiser, who bets. The small blind folds and you raise representing an ace and hoping the late-position raiser has a hand like J-10 or Q-J or 5-5 and decides to give up. He calls, though, and now you miss the turn.

Some players check here, hoping for the "inverse free card play" whereby their opponent may check behind them, fearing they are trying to check-raise again. Many timid opponents will actually give a free card here with a hand like J-J or Q-Q, hoping to get to a one-bet showdown. I am not a fan of the inverse free card play, as I prefer to put pressure on opponents who have J-J in this situation, but there are many opponents who will never release a pair. So when should you check?

- ♠ If you are viewed as a tricky player, your opponent will call you down with anything decent, but may distrust your check.
- ♠ If you are up against a timid calling station, who will check behind you, but never fold a good hand.
- ♠ If your opponent is a tricky, aggressive player who may be waiting to raise you (but maybe then your semi-bluff was not such a good idea).

Checking violates the principle that, if you are going to call, you are generally better off betting. Therefore check only if one (or more) of the three exceptions above exists. If none of them do, or you are not sure, betting is the better option.

2. You raised for value with a draw and missed

Again you are in the blind, this time with A♥-2♥. You call an early position raise after four other callers, so six of you see the flop, which comes K♥-8♥-7♣. You check and the original raiser bets, three players call, and you raise for value since you will make the nuts nearly one-third of the time and are getting at least 2-to-1 and possibly 4-to-1 on your raise (unless the raiser three-bets and everyone folds). Now the turn is a 6♦. Should you bet here?

I don't see why. Assuming your raise got a few callers, you can't possibly win the pot with a bet. After you miss the turn, you are a 4-to-1 dog to make you hand, so unless you will get four-way action, every incremental bet you put in will have −EV. You will need to put them in due to pot odds, but you would rather put in no bets or one, and the only way to accomplish that is to check.

3. You were semi-bluffing or raising for value, and hit

This is the same as the cases above except you made your hand. You will generally bet here, but are there exceptions?

If your hand is well hidden, and your opponent is very aggressive, it may pay to check and call on the turn and check-raise the river on occasion, just to slow him down. In Internet play, this play works well against auto-bettors.

4. Your big hand became bigger

Sometimes you check-raise with a hand like two pair or a set, and your hand improves to a full house or better. When should you slowplay?

The answer depends on the number of opponents, how loose they are, your image, and the number of draws on the board. Here are some cases:

- ♠ *With one timid opponent,* you want to make sure to get at least one big bet. If he tends to respect your check-raise on the flop and fold to your bet unless he has a decent hand, you need to be careful. If there are few draws on the board you can check, hoping your broken wing act will gain you a crying call on the river. If draws are present, bet and hope he has one that will keep him playing.

- ♠ *With one aggressive opponent* who will almost always bet if you check, go ahead and let him.

- ♠ *With more than one opponent,* you should bet even without draws present, because one of them will probably have enough of a hand to call you down.

5. You thought you had the best hand, but the turn was bad for you

This situation was discussed with an example in Chapter 18. We will look at two more examples here.

Example 1

This time you are the big blind with J♣-9♣. After two limpers the button raises, and you call, as do the limpers. The flop is 9♠-6♦-3♣, and you check to the raiser who bets. You raise to protect your vulnerable hand, and the limper folds. The button calls. Now the turn is the K♥. This can't make you happy, but should you bet or check?

In general, bet. Your opponent may have a king, but he also may have many hands that do not contain one, such as A-Q, A-J, A-10, Q-J, J-10, 8-8, or 7-7. If you check, and he checks, you have given a free card to all those hands. If you check, and he bets, you can't be sure he has a king because he may just bet because you checked.

If your opponent is straightforward, you can bet and fold if he raises. The real problem comes against clever, aggressive opponents who will decide to represent a king whether they have one or not. These opponents are tough to play against from out of position, but most of them will also bet automatically if you check. The odds favor checking and calling the turn, hoping that this is one of the times he does not hold a king or that you draw out.

Example 2

It is even possible that the turn card is bad enough and your read good enough that you can check and fold the turn after check-raising the flop. Here is such a situation from a $30-$60 game I played.

On this hand, I had developed what I call a "presumptive tell" on a tall bearded player (TBP). Once, when he raised before the flop, he looked around to assess his position, see where the blinds were, and then put his chips in. On another occasion, he just raised when it was his turn without looking around at all. On this scanty evidence, I theorized that, when he held a good raising hand, he knew he was going to raise and just did it. With a marginal raising hand, he paused to assess the situation and confirm in his mind that raising was a good idea.

I was in the big blind with A♥-4♣. After three folds, TBP did his look around tell and then raised. I took that show to mean a mediocre raising hand, perhaps a medium pair or a hand like K-J offsuit. All folded to the button, who called.

He was another stranger, but he was young and had seemed fairly active in the previous hour. I had designated him in my mind as an "action player (AP)", a guy who wanted to participate in many pots. He was fairly aggressive, so I thought he would three-bet with a big pair or big ace. In fact, I assumed he was type of action player who reraised with any pair in that spot.

The small blind folded, and I had to decide whether to call. Normally, that decision is easy. I strongly dislike playing ace-rag, I dislike it even more when I have to call a raise, and I truly hate it when I have to call a raise out of position. I almost always muck this hand without a second thought after a raise and a cold call. This time was different, however, as my reads convinced me that I likely had the best hand. I called the raise.

The flop was A♠-6♣-3♠ so I had top pair and a terrible kicker. If I was right, though, I had the only pair of aces at the table. I don't always check to the raiser in this spot, but in this case I wanted TBP to bet so I could trap AP for an extra bet if he called. So I checked and TBP dutifully bet, which he almost certainly would do with any hand. Now, however, AP raised!

What was happening? I came up with four possibilities:

- ♠ He had a medium pair and raised to eliminate me and find out from subsequent action whether his hand was good.

- ♠ He held an ace.

- ♠ He had a flush draw.

- ♠ He had 66 or 33 and flopped a set.

None of these made a lot of sense to me. If he had one of the first two holdings, he most likely would have reraised before the flop, being an action player. If he had flopped a set, he would probably wait for the turn to put his raise in, and he still might have three-bet pre-flop with that holding. If he had the flush draw, he might be better off calling and letting me in to help pay for his draw. The flush draw seemed likeliest, though, so I three-bet from the blind. TBP folded, so that took care of that concern, and AP called.

The turn was a disappointing 10♠, completing the flush draw if he had one. In fact, I was rapidly running out of hands I could beat. If my flush-draw assumption was correct, he had just drawn out on me. If he didn't, then I was wrong earlier, and he was ahead all the time. In either event, it was bye-bye Barry. I checked the turn, he bet, and I folded.

My fold elicited an unusual reaction from AP. He stared at me in disbelief. Perhaps he never saw a sequence in which a player three-bet the flop and then check-folded on the turn. He slowly turned over first the spade king and then the spade queen, while staring me down.

His actions made me happy, of course, because it confirmed that I had played the hand well, at least post-flop (I am still not that happy about playing the A-4 to begin with, even though it was probably the best hand). I put in the maximum amount of money when I was ahead, and folded immediately when I was drawing dead.

NOTE: Just because you check-raised the flop does not mean you must bet out or even continue to play.

6. Nothing happened, and you think you still have the best hand

Sometimes you check-raise believing you have the best hand, and nothing much happens to change your conviction. Is there a time you should check?

Though rare, the answer is yes. Once again, you need an aggressive opponent and something on the board he can represent.

Example

Here is a quick example. I held J-J in the big blind. After one limper, a very aggressive player raised. I called because I did not think I could get this limper to fold if I three-bet. The flop was 9-9-4 and I check-raised the raiser. The limper folded, and the raiser called. A three came on the turn. I felt that the raiser had very little, as he was raising with great frequency, though he could have me beat. I was sure he would bet if I checked, and was afraid he would fold if I bet.

I check-called the turn and check-called the river when a deuce came. He showed down A-2, so I took down the pot, which included the two extra big bets he donated after my turn check.

You need to be aware of opportunities like this to score extra bets from frequent bluffers.

Check-raising the flop does not mean you must bet the turn, even if you believe you have the best hand. Analyze each situation and vary your play among betting, check-raising, and check-calling. If you can do this, you will show more profit and keep your opponents off-balance when you do check after you check-raise.

You checked the flop, and no one bet

When everyone checks, you can usually assume that no one has much. There are exceptions, however, so let's talk about them first.

If there are one or two callers and a pre-flop raiser, beware if the raiser checks in late position. Perhaps the raiser has little or nothing and is just giving up, but don't believe that unless you have seen him give up in this spot before. Many players who flop a big hand after raising will check the flop almost reflexively. They hope the other players either make enough to pay them off, think some second-best hand just became better, or just bluff into a pot that nobody seems to want.

This is not necessarily the case if the pre-flop raiser has been called several places. For example, if there were four limpers and the button raised with 10♥-10 ♣, he may well check after everyone checks to him if the flop comes A♠-Q♠-4♦.

For the remainder of this analysis, assume that the pre-flop raiser is not trapping, or that nobody raised and everyone checked the flop. You were in early position and checked, so you were in one of these situations:

1. You had nothing.
2. You had something, but were not sure where you stood.
3. You planned to check-raise.

1. You had nothing

When everyone checks the flop, and you are first to act, you are in an excellent bluffing position on the turn. Nobody can be certain that you were not trying to check-raise on the flop, so your check does not deny power. Your decision whether to bluff depends on the following:

- ♠ The turn card.
- ♠ The number of opponents.
- ♠ Your opponents' tendencies.
- ♠ Pot size.
- ♠ Your image.

The turn card

The less likely this card is to have helped the enemy, the more often you should bet at it. This is a particularly true if the board pairs, so if no one had anything before, they cannot have improved. This card will frighten your opponents, because you could have checked for a raise or had top pair with a weak kicker. If they don't hold trips, they may be drawing nearly dead if you do.

Example

Two players limp, and the small blind folds. You are in the big blind with Q♥-9♠. The flop is 8♦-4♣-2♥. You check, and the other two players check behind you. Let's see how you should respond to various turn cards.

- ♠ Below a ten: Bet. It is unlikely this has helped anyone's hand.

- ♠ Ten or jack: Check and fold. Tens and jacks are too dangerous to bet, since many players like to limp with those cards.

- ♠ Queen: This is good news and bad news. The good news is you have made a pair. The bad news is anyone else with a queen will have a better kicker. Bet, but be prepared to give up quickly if you get raised.

- ♠ King: This is not a bad card. In general, limpers are more likely to have queens, jacks, and tens than kings, because more players raise with good kings and fold bad ones. It is definitely worth a bet.

- ♠ Ace: Aces are more problematic. If the players in your game tend to limp with any ace, check and fold. If they tend to raise with ace-good-kicker and fold with ace-bad-kicker, bet.

This play works best when the pot is small, as do most bluffs. Even if your opponents suspect you are bluffing, they will generally not want to bother with such a small amount of money unless they have something.

The number of opponents

It's hard to bluff multiple opponents. Just because everyone checked does not mean they all missed entirely, so someone who flopped middle or bottom pair and just wants to see what you have may call you down. Most bluffs into four or more opponents are semi-bluffs, so you need a draw if you get called or raised.

Example

You are in the small blind with 8♠-5♠. Four players limp, you call, and the big blind checks. On a flop of 9♠-4♦-3♣ you check as does everyone else. Bet if the turn card is a low spade or a six, because these cards now give you a good draw. The combination of winning the pot now or getting called and making your hand makes this play worthwhile. Without a good draw, give up quietly and wait for a better spot.

Even if you pair the eight or five, betting is not that good a play. Check and see what develops. If there is a bet and call, give up. If everyone checks to the last player and he bets, check-raise unless he would never bluff.

Your opponents' tendencies

I include this because occasionally you will observe an opponent who loves to bluff at "orphan pots". If you are up to making a risky play, you are better off checking the turn in good bluffing situations and allowing him to bluff at it. Then, if everyone folds, check-raise.

You can't do this every time the situation develops with that player, or he will catch on. Do it once every two to three times to make a nice profit on his predictability.

Watch out for calling stations. They hate to bet, but love to call. They may check top or middle pair on the flop, not because they are tricky, but because they are being their usual selves. Of course, they may also have nothing, but their presence makes bluffing less attractive.

Pot size

The bigger the pot, the higher the reward, but the more likely it is that someone will make a call. Tiny pots are frequently up for grabs because nobody wants to risk that much on them.

Take a look at the smallest possible pot. Everyone folds to the small blind who calls. The big blind checks. Both players now check the flop. If the small blind bets the turn, he is getting even money. He must win half the time to break even.

However, the big blind is now facing a pot-sized bet and, unless he was trapping, he cannot have that much. Even if he has a draw with overcards, he is not getting the right price if the small blind has any sort of hand. He will not have that good a hand very often, so the small blind's bet should win often enough to show a profit even though he is frequently bluffing. Of course, some of the times he bets he will have at least a pair.

In large multiway pots, bluffing out of position is virtually impossible. Don't try it.

Your image

The tighter your image, the easier the turn bluff becomes. If you are seen as a frequent bluffer, trying to win with a well-known bluff play becomes harder as some opponents will either be suspicious enough to call you with ace high, or just try to make a counter-play with a bluff-raise.

2. You had something, but were not sure where you stood

You should have a much better idea now. You should bet unless the turn card is truly frightening. You may get curiosity calls from a player who suspects you are bluffing.

3. You planned to check-raise

Normally if your hand was good enough to check-raise, you will be happy to bet the turn. Be even more anxious to bet if the turn card brings likely draws.

However, some players will bet the turn with thin values once everyone checks the flop and everyone checks the turn to them. A player with middle or even bottom pair may promote it to "likely best hand" if no one else bets. Also, many pre-flop raisers who check the flop will almost always bet the turn for value if checked to again. They hope their play looks like they were trapping on the flop and everyone will fold, or that somehow their A-K or underpair is good since no one had enough to bet. If you check again, you may get to check-raise the turn with the best hand.

One other player to watch for is the one mentioned above who bets when he believes the pot is up for sale. Make sure you let him bet. If other players are aware of his tendency, you may even get extra action before you spring your trap.

You bet the flop, and no one raised

In general, you would keep betting since you took the lead, and that is often the best plan. To take a more in depth look, let's look at the four reasons you could have had to bet the flop:

1. You had a big hand.
2. You had a mediocre hand.
3. You had a draw.
4. You were bluffing.

1. You had a big hand

In general, if you have a big hand, you should keep betting. This is particularly true if you are out of position, since you don't want to risk giving a free card that may beat you. If you have aggressive opponents, you could try for a check-raise, but these opponents just called, so they may not be feeling aggressive now.

The only reason to reconsider would be if a scary card hit, and you now fear a raise. Most commonly, this is an overcard or flush card. Let's look at both:

Overcard example

You raised in middle position with J♥-J♣ and got two callers behind you. The flop was 9♦-8♠-6♣. You bet, and one player called. Now the turn is the K♥. Should you bet into the overcard?

Yes, you should. You may no longer be best, of course, but checking gives away too many free cards. Your opponent may have a king, but he may also have an ace, a small pair, or even a straight draw with hand like A♣-7♣. Even if you have several opponents, you could easily still have the best hand, as some opponents with 5♦-5♠ hope you have a hand like A-Q or A-J and will pay you off.

Flush card example

Again you raised with J♥-J♣ and got two callers. This time the flop came K♥-8♦-3♦. You bet, the next player folded, and the button called.

The turn is the 4♦, putting a three-flush on the board. Now what?

There is a chance your opponent has a king, but he might have raised with it. There is also a chance he has the flush. If there were four or more opponents, you could check now, planning to fold, but with only one you still need to represent the best hand.

If your opponent is straightforward, bet and fold if he raises. If your opponent is tricky, you may need to check and call twice. You will lose two more bets those times when you have the worst hand, but that can't be helped sometimes. If instead you bet and get raised by the tricky player, you still can't be sure where you stand. If you check, you will pick off enough bluffs and mistaken value bets (with hands like 7♣-7♠) to make your situation worth continuing.

2. You had a mediocre hand

Sometimes you bet a mediocre hand like middle pair to try to win the pot and perhaps determine where you stand. If you get called in several places, you should usually stop betting. Against one player, keep betting unless the board has no draws, and the opponent has no logical hand that you can beat. The more draws the board shows, the more likely that your opponent is in fact drawing, and you need to bet the best hand and avoid giving free cards. Here is an example.

Example

You held 6♣-6♦ in the small blind and called with two other callers and the big blind. The flop was 8♦-3♠-3♣ and you decided to bet because, if you had the best hand, you could not afford to give free cards. If the big blind folded, and one or two limpers called, you should now bet the turn because they probably have overcards. If a strong player in the big blind called, give up on the turn. He would not have called here with overcards because he had to fear a raise behind him, and he had to worry that you could have a three. If he held a hand like J♠-8♣ for top pair, he would have raised to eliminate the two limpers who could draw out to beat his vulnerable hand. Weak players call with overcards from the big blind, so you should keep betting in that case.

If instead the flop was Q♥-Q♣-5♦ and anyone called you, you should generally give up. Your limping opponents cannot have two overcards, and there are no draws. Someone has a queen here, and it is not you.

If the flop was 8♠-8♣-7♠, bet the turn if a non-straight, non-flush card hits, as the chances are your opponents have a draw instead of a made hand.

3. You had a draw

If your draw hits, bet. Your hand is disguised by the fact that you bet the flop with a draw instead of a made hand, and opponents who can beat some of those possible made hands will probably pay you off.

You may be tempted to check-raise, but to do that, someone else has to bet. Because the turn card completes a draw, your opponents may think that you are checking a good hand on the turn, fearing they made the draw. If they reason this way, they may check behind you. Since you want someone to bet here, it should be you.

If you miss your draw, decide what the chances are of having the opponents give up on the turn. If you are going to call a bet anyway, you should generally bet. If there are several opponents, and the turn card was a bad one, check and hope for a free card. If there is a bet, assess your pot odds in light of the bad turn card.

Example

You hold 7♦-6♦ in the big blind and call after one limper and a raise from the button. The flop hits 9♦-8♣-3♠. You bet, and both players call. If the turn is the 9♥, bet because you have represented a nine. If your opponents have overcards, they will fear they are drawing dead and fold. If the turn is the 2♠, bet because your opponents may have taken one off to see if they could hit an overcard cheaply.

On the other hand, if the turn is the J♥, give up. You no longer have a true open-ended straight draw, as a ten would give anyone with a queen a higher straight. Also, limpers could have already made a better straight or have a jack and raise.

4. You were bluffing

Assume you have only one opponent, because running a pure bluff on two or more is rare. If you bluff and get called, give up. The pot is small (with only one opponent), and he probably has something to call you with. He has position and could be slowplaying a big hand or just calling with something mediocre with which he does not want to risk a raise. Unless the turn card looks like it may convince him to fold a made hand, give up. You tried, and it did not work.

Remember, by betting and then check-folding, you also encourage your opponent to make a loose play against you when you have a very good hand. If you have check-folded the turn a time or two, remember to check-raise this opponent later in the session as you have trained him to bet thin values "knowing" you will fold.

You bet the flop, got raised and you called

Many players react automatically in this position, simply checking to the raiser on the turn. Resist this temptation, and make a thoughtful decision instead. You still may end up checking most of the time, but you will also bet when it is right to do so. In this case, we need to look only at three reasons for your play, as we do not need to consider the times when you bluffed and called a raise.

1. You had a big hand.
2. You had a mediocre hand.
3. You had a draw.

1. You had a big hand

Since you bet a big hand and then called a raise, you probably were planning to check-raise the turn. Presumably, you based your decision on these criteria:

♠   Number of opponents (higher = three-bet the flop.)
♠   Vulnerability of your hand (more = three-bet the flop.)
♠   Probability opponent wants a free card (higher = three-bet the flop.)
♠   Chances a scare card will hit (higher = three-bet the flop.)
♠   Aggression of raiser (higher = check-raise the turn.)
♠   Your image (aggressive = three-bet the flop.)

Regardless of what comes on the turn, check to fulfil your plan.

2. You had a mediocre hand

You bet out, were raised, and you called. If this chapter has taught you anything, it should be that you do not automatically check to the raiser on the turn (or at any other time). Let's look at some cases that you may decide to bet:

1. You improved.
2. You suspect your opponent wants a free card.
3. The turn card helps you to represent a big hand.

1) You improved

Assuming you have now improved to a hand better than the one your opponent is representing, you have to decide whether to try for a check-raise. I generally prefer betting to check-raising for several reasons:

217

- ♠ You may get raised again, in which case you can three-bet.
- ♠ Check-raising may cause an opponent with a marginal hand to fold, as he realizes you were trapping him. Betting may induce enough uncertainty to get you paid off.
- ♠ Betting provides balance for the bluffs you may want to make in this situation, which will be covered later. If you always check-raise with a good hand, betting as a bluff loses credibility. Naturally, this holds true only if your opponents are observant, but those are exactly the kind of opponents you can bluff.
- ♠ He may check behind you, netting you no bets on this round.

If there are several players to trap between the pre-flop raiser and you, check-raising is more attractive. If you are heads-up, I suggest you bet, even though check-raising seems cleverer and more fun.

2) You suspect your opponent wants a free card

This is always a tough situation. If your opponent wants a free card, you should bet. If he has a big hand, you will get raised again. A straightforward opponent will play this way, and you should therefore bet, preventing the free card and allowing you to fold if you get raised.

Unfortunately, many opponents are either aggressive or tricky. If you cannot trust your opponent enough to know that you should fold if he raises again, checking is better than betting and paying off all the way if raised. You will have to make the decision whether to check and fold or call all the way based on the probability your opponent is either bluffing or making thin value bets after you check. There are many disadvantages in being out of position, and this is one of them.

3) The turn card helps you to represent a big hand

The difference between this case and the previous one is that here you are very unlikely to be raised, assuming you would bet that big hand if you had actually made it. As a general rule, if you can bet and not get raised on a hand you would be calling anyway, bet. You may win it right there.

3. You had a draw

You bet your draw and got raised. Now on the turn one of two things can happen:

1. You made your draw.
2. You missed.

1) You made your draw

The temptation to check-raise is high, and if you can trap a few players for extra bets, check-raising is a good idea. If the raiser is aggressive, you can also check-raise.

Betting into the raiser may cost you a bet if he folds and would have bet had you checked, but it increases your credibility if you do get called to the river (or, even better, get raised at some point). Your willingness to bet good hands will pay off when you bluff, as in the next case.

2) You missed

Here is where all of that betting with good hands makes you more money. A single opponent raised pre-flop, and you called in the blind. You were heads-up, flopped a draw, and bet. He raised, and you called.

Many players who raise pre-flop also raise on the flop to keep control of the hand, either to play aggressively or to get a free card with A-K or A-Q. If your opponent could be such a player, and if the turn card is either innocuous or could have helped your hand, I suggest you occasionally bet. Even though you are still on a draw, this bet looks like you either:

- ♠ Had a decent hand that improved, or
- ♠ Just hit your hand, or
- ♠ Had a decent hand and put your opponent on overcards or a draw.

Betting mimics the play in which you are afraid of giving your opponent a free card, even though you would really prefer a free card yourself. You are going to call anyway, so betting does not cost you anything unless he was going to check (in which case he may now fold), or he raises. If he does raise, call and hope to draw out.

The number of times he folds makes this play a worthwhile addition to your poker arsenal. Remember, you can make this tricky semi-bluff only if you are known as a player who frequently bets his good hands on the turn. If opponents believe you always check-raise good hands on the turn, this play will lack credibility.

If you have more than one opponent, then semi-bluffing again makes little sense. Check and hope for a free card. If someone bets, as will usually happen, you need to assess your chances of making your hand in terms of pot and implied odds, and the chances your hand will be good if you make it. This is just sound poker, but many players forget to count the pot and a make a correct mathematical decision, which is what this situation calls for.

You bet the flop, got raised, and you reraised

Generally, when you reraise on the flop, you do so with the intention of betting the turn. We will discuss exceptions below.

As before, for completeness, we will look at the following reasons why you may have bet the flop:

1. You had a big hand.
2. You had a mediocre hand.
3. You had a draw.
4. You were bluffing.

1. You had a big hand

Heads-up you will rarely find a reason to check the turn. There are always a few, such as you had Q-Q and three-bet a flop of K-Q-10. A jack on the turn may make you stop and think, but you should just bull ahead with a bet and worry about it if you get raised. You would call and have a tough decision on the river if you do not fill up, but checking the turn does not give an opponent holding K-10 a chance to fold, and allows him a free chance to beat you.

Multiway, these four-card straights and flushes become much more problematic. Say you open-raise in early position with K♥-K♦. One middle position and two late position players call, and the blinds fold. The flop of 9♠-8♣-7♦ does not thrill you, but you bet, one player calls, and the next one raises. The last player folds, and you reraise. Both remaining players call.

The turn card is the 6♣, putting an open-ended straight on the board. Nothing says someone has to have a ten here, but betting would force you to face a raise most of the time, with a good chance that you are drawing dead. Checking works, with a plan to call one bet and fold to a bet and a raise. If the turn were the 10♣ instead, checking and folding would be more reasonable. More players call raises with jacks than they do with tens. Correct or not, opponents call raises with A-J, K-J, Q-J, J-10, and J-9 suited.

2. You had a mediocre hand

You could have several reasons to reraise with a mediocre hand. The two most common are:

1. Your opponent may be trying for a free card, and
2. You are trying to eliminate callers.

1. Your opponent may be trying for a free card

Most of the time when you are raised on the flop, you will not be sure whether you are ahead and your opponent is trying for a free card, or you are behind. Reraising and betting out can help you to determine which one is correct. If your opponent needed a free card, betting ensures he does not get it. If he has you beat, he may raise to alert you to the fact.

This is one of several areas in which playing out of position is so difficult. If you just call his flop raise and check the turn, you are giving away too many free cards. If you always reraise and bet the turn, you are often paying a premium to play the worst hand.

One of the keys here is what sort of opponent you have. If he had a good hand, would he raise or wait for the turn? Many opponents wait to raise after the bets double, making his flop raise suspicious and your reraise and turn bet more plausible. This is especially true in aggressive games, where opponents often raise the flop to retake control even with marginal hands.

The texture of the flop and the nature of the turn card will guide you on the turn. If you put your opponent on either a better hand or a draw, and the draw gets there, check and fold.

2. You are trying to eliminate callers

This situation is more difficult, so an example may help. You raise in middle position with 10♥-10♣. In an unwelcome development, three callers come in behind you, and the big blind calls as well. The flop is J♣-8♦-7♦. The big blind checks, you bet and, after two players call, the button raises. The big blind folds, and you reraise to eliminate possible overcards and gutshot draws from the remaining two callers. You may be ahead or behind here, but if you can get two players out, your equity in the remaining pot increases when you are ahead. If you succeed, bet the turn heads-up. If one or both call, you are almost certainly in trouble and should check-fold the turn unless you pick up a straight or a set on the turn.

3. You had a draw

You reraise with a draw under several circumstances, the most common of which are:

1. You had a huge draw.
2. You were semi-bluffing heads-up.

In almost all circumstances, having gone this far, bet the turn. If the pot is multiway and you are sure you can't win with a bet, you may want to try for an "inverse free card". Heads-up you are better off continuing the bluff unless your opponent, once he calls your flop raise, always calls to the end.

4. You were bluffing

I realize some of you think it is unlikely you would reraise bluff, but it certainly is better than calling. If you decide it is worth representing something, typically either an ace or a card matching a small pair on board, continuing your bluff is the only way to win.

This play is advanced. Make it only if you know your opponent quite well, and your image is such that he knows you would play the hand exactly this way if you actually held it.

The flop is 9-5-5 and you, holding Q-8, bet the flop and reraise when he raises. You can do this only if you also play that way if your hand were A-5. Many players try to represent a five here, but if they actually have one, they wait and try to check-raise the turn. More importantly, your opponent must believe you would play a five this way whether you would or not, and he must be capable of laying a decent hand down.

Conclusion

♠ Playing out of position is tough. You are often guessing about the right play.

♠ No matter what your plan was on the flop, you need to evaluate the impact of the turn card before you play.

♠ Don't automatically check to the player who raised on the flop. Always think about both of your options.

♠ Bluffing from out of position has more credibility than bluffing in position.

♠ Exploit overly aggressive players. Check and give them a chance to make an error.

♠ Balance is critical. If you are going to bluff in some circumstances, you must bet a good hand in the same situation.

♠ When you make a big hand on the turn, betting is often better than check-raising. Take the time to decide and don't automatically go for check-raises.

Part Two: Stages

On the River

Chapter Twenty-Three

River Play Overview

The river is different from all the other streets. There are no more draws. Implied odds no longer have any meaning. One player has the best hand and will take the pot unless he folds. The only things to discuss are:

- ♠ How to make the most money if you are ahead,
- ♠ How (and when) to make the best hand fold if you don't have it, and,
- ♠ Sadly, how to lose the least when you are behind.

Aside from bluffs, river betting comes down to winning or losing an extra bet or two, except for those cases that you bet with a losing hand and the other player incorrectly folds.

In this chapter, we will cover the following topics:

- ♠ Value betting.
- ♠ Inducing bluffs.
- ♠ Implementing your plan.
- ♠ Out-of-position play.

♠ In-position play.

♠ Folding.

♠ Multiway pots.

Value betting

Several texts offer accurate mathematical models regarding betting on the river, particularly heads-up. I would like to extend this topic beyond the mathematical into the effect your bet has on the opponent if you are heads-up.

First, let's define "value bet". It is a bet made on the river by a hand that may or may not be best. You hope you have the best hand often enough that the calls you collect when you win outweigh the losses you take when you lose. Remember, the winner of the pot is already decided; you are simply jousting for an extra bet or two at the end. These extra bets add significantly to the expert player's profits.

Never be disappointed that your value bet is not called. One possibility is that your opponent mistook your bet as showing a better hand, and folded a winner. In this case, you win an entire pot you could not have won any other way. Another possibility is that your opponent folded a loser, but is now bothered because he cannot be certain you were not bluffing.

Consider that you bet on the river, and the opponent goes into a long study. Already this bet has done a lot of good:

♠ Your opponent clearly thinks he has a tough decision and may make the wrong one occasionally, or even frequently.

♠ He is wasting brain energy on this decision that he could have conserved if you had not bet.

There are other psychological benefits as well. If the opponents fold, even correctly, you now create some uncertainty in their minds. You did not show your hand. Maybe you were bluffing. If you bet three or four times and win with no call, the suspicion grows deeper, even if you were simply betting the best hand. Now, when you bet the fifth time with a decent hand, you may get called by someone with a very weak hand who simply cannot stand it any more and wants to look you up. My favorite thing to hear in poker is, "I know I'm beat, but I'm going to call you anyway."

Even when you bet a marginal hand and lose, there is long-term value. Opponents who see you make thin value bets on the river are more likely to pay off your good hands, and if you play a solid game, you will be betting good hands most of the time.

There is yet another consideration. People are conditioned to call on the river. They understand that their opponent will be bluffing some of the time, and they must call with any hand that can beat a bluff. So your value bets will get called a surprising number of times by players who have almost nothing, but hope this is the time you have absolutely nothing.

Clearly, you should not bet for value when the only hands that can call you must have you beat. In a game like limit hold'em, however, opponents are free to imagine all sorts of holdings or invent bluffs they can beat. The probability that you will be called only when you are beat goes down considerably. I have seen people who were *bluffing* get called and win the pot. You never really know what an opponent might put you on, and what hand he will decide he just has to call with.

Here are a couple of examples:

Example 1

After a weak limper enters, a decent player who is also a very frequent bluffer raises. I have A-K and three-bet. All fold back to the limper who calls, as does the initial raiser. The flop is Q-8-3 rainbow. Both players check to me, and, because I hate queens when I hold A-K and because I can make a play later with position if I feel like I should, I check behind them. In general, I would bet here, and I recommend that you do as well, but this a play I make for variation, and I happened to make it here. Now, an eight comes on the turn, putting a second diamond on the board. The weak player checks, and the next guy bets. This means absolutely nothing, so I raise to get the limper out. Remarkably, he calls two cold quickly. The other guy calls as well.

OK, what's happening? If the weak player had a queen, he would have led on the turn. If he had an eight, he would have reraised (or at least thought about it). Most likely he has picked up a diamond draw and wants to see if he makes it (or he has quads, but I dismiss this).

The river is an offsuit five. Both players check. Now normally I check A-K here, as it is hard to believe anyone can call with a worse hand. However, since someone might think I have represented a set of queens (and I would have played a set of queens this way), the weak player could lay down something like 4♦ 3♦, which beats me. Also, the original raiser might lay down an A-K, which would otherwise be splitting the pot. I bet out so that no one wins or ties by accident.

The weak player folds, and the other guy calls. I show my A-K, and it wins. Actually, I thought it was likely the best hand of the two of us, but I did not think it would be if called. He shows ace-ten, and tells me he "knew I had nothing". He also tells me he should have raised. I agree (but do not tell him this), but I'm not sure I would have folded, given what I think of his play. Of course, that's easier to say once I have seen his hand, but what hand could he have to check-raise the river that would have flat called my raise on the turn?

Example 2

Four players (I am not in the hand) check the turn of 10-10-6-4. The river card is a nine, and the first player checks. The next player bets and gets two callers. Now the first player folds.

The bettor turns over pocket threes. They win! The next caller had pocket deuces and the over-caller had A-K (what was he thinking?). The folder now complains that she held a four and folded the best hand. She is wondering how she could have made the second overcall (she couldn't, of course.)

Notice that the guy with pocket threes could not have won any other way. And he won the max.

I am not saying that you should bet pocket threes in this example. But this hand makes the point that when you think nobody can call you who does not have you beat, you may be surprised at what some opponents think they can or should call with. And someone may fold the winner as well.

Value betting also has excellent psychological advantages, which play into the *Illusion of Action*. If you bet on the river, an opponent calls, and you win, that's great. If he folds and you win, that's good too. Perhaps you should not have bet because, if called, you may have lost, but the fact is you won a pot without a showdown. These repeated bets enhance your loose image, which gains you calls and increases the FUD factor.

I do need to put in a word of caution about value betting. Most of the time that you make a value bet, you are planning to fold if raised. This plan works fine against most players, who fold with nothing, call with something, and raise with the near nuts. As you start playing higher-limit games, however, you will meet an occasional player, typically an excellent card reader, who will raise your value bets when he feels they are, in fact, value bets.

They may be bluff raises, or even "value raises", hoping you have a hand close in value to his and will not be able to call, or will call and lose. These are tough players, which is why they are playing high, and you need to be careful around them. Value betting does not work as well, and you may lose earnings because you are now checking some decent hands that you would prefer to get paid off. Balance and FUD are key because those principles can thwart even excellent card readers. Tough games require tough countermeasures.

Inducing bluffs

In many ways, inducing bluffs is the opposite of value betting. To induce a bluff, you need to be out of position and have a hand with at least enough value to win a showdown. Then you need to check it, foregoing the possible crying call, to get your opponent to bet a hand he would have folded had you bet. If he has a hand with some showdown value, but is worse than yours, you have lost a bet, as he may simply check it down behind you.

If you learn to love value betting, you will not induce many bluffs, as you will bet most of your decent hands. You do need to learn when you should try to induce a bluff, so let's look at some advantages and then some things to look for.

The primary advantage of attempting to induce bluffs is that you may win a bet you could not have won any other way. However, there are few meta-game[9] advantages as well.

If your opponent sees that you will occasionally check a decent hand in hopes of getting him to bluff off some money, he may cut down his bluffing frequency. This works well for you in that he becomes more predictable (you can trust his river bets to have value). It also works well when he gives up on a hand that he might have tried to bluff someone else with, and you win a whole pot by default because you had given up as well, but your nothing beats his nothing.

You need to look for certain qualities in your opponent before trying this play. First, and most obviously, he must be willing to bluff. Do not assume this. To check a decent hand hoping for a bluff, you must have seen this player bluff before.

Second, the river card must look like it bothers you, at least a little. If you have been betting your Q-J into a K♣-J♦-7♣-5♥ board and the 2♥ hits, you would have no reason to check unless you were semi-bluffing with a hand like Q-10 and were now giving up. He has no reason to bluff even an ace-high hand, though he may try it with a hand like Q-10. Would you check now with your Q-J? No, because if he has a king, you are going to lose a bet whether you check or bet. If he has a jack, you want to bet for value. But consider what happens if the river card is a nine. Now you may look to him like a guy who was betting a hand like A-10 and will fold if he bets.

Ironically, if the river card could make a flush, like the 6♣, you are better off making the value bet. This is because he will assume you checked because you are afraid of the flush, are planning to call a bet, and were afraid you might be raised. Some players will think, "Oh, I will bet and represent a flush, and he will fold," but they are in the minority in tough games.

---

[9] "Meta-game" refers to the overall session or, in the case of players you play with often, the long series of sessions you will play with them. Hands do not stand alone, and plays you make now reverberate throughout the meta-game.

Implementing your plan

The river is not a stand-alone street. You should not have gotten there without a plan. By the time it is your turn on the river, you probably have a good idea what is happening. Either your plan is in place, or something surprising has happened (an unexpected card or opponent's action).

Example

Here is an example of a plan and the temptation to change it. After the under the gun player limps, you raise on the button with K♠-10♦. The limper is a loose player, but can be aggressive after the flop. The small blind, also loose, and the limper call. The flop is K♣-Q♥-6♣. Both check, you bet, SB raises and UTG calls. You decide to call intending to raise the turn for a free showdown if a blank hits the turn. This seems like a reasonable line, as UTG is either drawing or has a huge hand. If he raises the SB on the turn, you may be able to get away from your hand (if he just has good hand, he would three-bet the flop to get you out rather than give you a cheap look at the turn when you may hold be a pair or A-Q or even A-J). The turn is a blank looking 2♥. Sure enough, SB bets, UTG calls, you raise, and they both call. Now the river is the J♠ and they both check to you. Is this a good time to make a value bet?

I love value betting more than most, but the answer here is, "No." Your plan was to raise for a free showdown, so follow it. You already made your "value bet" when you raised the turn. Not only is a jack not a very good card for you, but your opponents may well be lying in wait for your bet. Take a look and see who wins.

Out-of-position play

On the first three streets, the player in position is generally the aggressor. Pre-flop, players on the button find all kinds of reasons to raise in a variety of situations. Similarly, on the flop, most bets and raises come from players in position, whether they are steals, value bets, free card tries, or player elimination plays. On the turn, players in position raise with made hands, draws, bluffs, and moderate hands willing to call in a showdown. Out-of-position players rarely raise without a huge hand.

On the river this role seems to change, and the burden of aggression suddenly falls upon the out-of-position player. If you are first to act, you may never get another chance, as the in-position players can end the hand at any time. If you want to get money into the pot, this may be the only chance you get.

You hold 10♥-10♣ and raise pre-flop from middle position. The button and big blind call. On a flop of 9♥-8♦-4♣, the blind checks, you bet, and the button raises. The blind folds, and you three-bet. On the turn of 5♦ it goes bet-call. Now the J♠ hits the river. Do you check or bet?

The jack is a bad card for you because many of the hands the button will call pre-flop and raise the flop have a jack in them. Hands like J-10 and Q-J are likely candidates. Nevertheless, you must bet. If he has a jack, you will check, he will bet and you will call. So you will lose a bet anyway. He is unlikely to raise with a jack, as you are more likely to have an overpair for your betting than specifically 10-10. If he has a hand like A-8 or 10-9 suited, he will check behind you if you check, and you will lose the river call you would probably get by betting. Only rarely will he hold a straight and raise you. You will probably pay off and lose two bets, but the net win for crying calls vs. miracle gutshots clearly favors betting.

Similarly, if you make a hand on the river, you should generally bet. Do not be seduced by the fact that the in-position player bet the flop and the turn, or that he raised the turn. Many players bet aggressively throughout the hand, planning to check on the river to see if their mediocre holding is good. They figure that if you were on a draw, their hand is good; if not, they will not waste a bet on the river. I know check-raising is fun and makes you look like a clever player. The problem is that no matter how much fun you have with the play, the sadness of turning over a great hand that collects no money on the river outweighs it.

There are other advantages to leading on the river when you have been passive all the way. Let's reverse roles for a moment and put you in position with, say, pocket jacks. You raised two limpers pre-flop, and they called. You bet the flop of K-10-5 and got one caller. You also bet the turn when an eight hit and were called. Now a nine hits on the river. This is a poor card for you as one of the most likely hands you could beat was Q-J. You may well decide to check it down. However, much to your annoyance, the other guy now bets. Does he have a king? Q-J? 10-9? All of these are plausible holdings you can't beat. Should you lay it down? The pot has almost eight big bets, so you are getting a good price to call. Part of the answer depends on who is betting, but most of the time you will call, and most of the time you will lose (which does not make calling wrong). And there goes a bet you may not have lost had the other guy checked.

You can see how that bet bothered you. You were suddenly confronted with a tough decision. Even if you held A-K, you could only call the river bet, as much as you might want to raise. Raising would re-open the betting for the out-of-position player to fold if he was bluffing, but he would three-bet if he had made a straight or (perhaps) two pair. That is way too risky for you, even though you had an easier call if you had A-K than you did with pocket jacks. And if you held A-Q, you could easily be forced to lay it down.

This little role reversal showed you how difficult life could be for the in-position player who was comfortably betting the flop and turn only to see the opponent unexpectedly bet the river. Tough in-position players often bet the turn whether they have much or not, hoping you will fold if you were just "taking one off," or you are on a draw and their modest values are actually best. Many of these players plan to check the river and see what's what.

As the player out of position, try to thwart that plan. Consider being the aggressor on the river whether you were betting all the way or just checking and calling. When you are out of position and planning to call a river bet, decide how often you can induce a bluff, or your opponent will bet a hand you can beat, as opposed to offering him a free showdown.

Betting is especially important when a scare card comes on the river. If it makes your hand, bet most of the time. But what if it does not make your hand, but you have a hand which my well be best and were planning to call a river bet? If you bet anyway, it is almost impossible for the opponent to raise because you may have made the hand the scare card represented. Against all but the toughest and most imaginative players, a raise by him shows that *he* made the hand, and you can fold. If he calls and you lose, you likely lost the same bet you were going to lose if you checked and called. If he is a timid player and always checks scare cards, then check with the hands you would like free showdowns with, and bet the others.

That brings us to the next point, which again is balance. If you ever want to bluff the river after check-calling all the way, you also have to bet the river when you have the goods. Habitual check-raisers may make an extra bet once in while when the in-position player has a hand worth betting, but they lose all credibility for the lead bluff, which can win a few whole pots.

To complicate matters, balance also requires that you check-raise once in a while, so your opponents realize that they cannot bet with impunity every time you check. Do not make this your default play, but wait for circumstances in which you have a very good chance that the in-position player will bet. You need to have an aggressive player who does not let scare cards bother him, a player who loves to make value bets on the end. Hey, someone like me! Yes, I would be a good candidate for a check-raise because I am less likely than most to check, as I like to put relentless pressure on my opponents. And, like all plays, it sometimes gets me into trouble. But the point here is that aggressive value bettors are the kind of people you want to attempt your check-raise against.

In an interesting hand, I was drawing out of position when a truly obvious scare card came on the river. It made just about everything, including my hand. In fact, it was so scary that almost nobody would check, as the in-position player would be too nervous to bet. But I was playing a frequent opponent who knew how I played. I checked, and he reasoned that there was no way I could check that card with any kind of hand because of the likelihood that he would check. Having worked that out, he confidently bet, and I check-raised! He glared for a while and paid me off. He then observed that he was the only player at the table I would have checked that hand against, as nobody else would think deeply enough to bet. He was correct, and it was a compliment to him, in a way, that he was a good enough player to think through the hand and make a value bet into that scare card.

In-position play

The in-position player always has the power to end the hand. He can check if checked to, and call if bet into. Unfortunately, many in-position players use this power as a way to take no chances whatsoever, avoiding the bluff, the value bet, and the raise. While it is true that any time the in-position player bets, he re-opens the betting for a raise, failure to remain aggressive costs a great deal of money.

Let's look at those options in more depth.

Bluffing

Often, the only way to win a pot is by bluffing. If you never bluff, you are giving away too much. As a general rule, bluff with your worst hands, the ones that cannot possibly win a showdown. Bluff only when you're heads-up (with the exception we will cover later) after betting sequences that at least give you hope that your opponent may fold.

For example, you have 8♠-7♠ on the button and limp in after three others. The small blind calls and the big blind raises. Everyone calls. On the flop of K♠-6♦-5♦, there is a bet, and the player on your right raises. With six outs to the nuts, a back-door flush draw and other chances, you call; everyone else folds to the bettor who calls. On the turn, J♣, it goes bet-you call-fold. Now the river is the 3♠. The bettor checks. What can this mean? Either he has a king and is going to call, or he has two diamonds, has missed, and is going to fold (other possibilities exist, of course, but these are the most likely). Go ahead and bet. There are 11 big bets in the pot, so if you win 9% of the time you break even for your investment. Yes, that also means you are likely to lose at least 90% of the time, but you will still win money in spots like this. Plus, if you happen to get called and show the hand, you will get action on real hands later, so the money will come back anyway. More *Illusion of Action* at work.

Value betting

The fact that your opponent has checked often means that either he has given up, or he has a mediocre hand and is going to call, though he hopes he will not have to make that decision. Force him to make it. I will not cover the advantages of value betting again, but they are at least as valid when you are in position as when you are out of position.

Some people believe they are even more valid because after all, the other player has checked so his hand cannot be great. True, but there is some indication that his hand cannot be terrible either, because he had a chance and did not bluff. In fact, a mistake many players make is value betting into a frequent bluffer who has checked. When he has nothing he bets, so checking and giving up his right to bluff generally means that he plans to call. You should still value bet your better hands, because he will be suspicious that this check has induced a bluff and will be predisposed to call. And of course, bluff with your worst hands if your opponent is capable of making a laydown.

Let's look at an example of a river value bet. In a weak game, a tight-aggressive player raises in middle position. You elect to call with A♥-Q♥, and the button and blinds call as well. On the flop of Q♠-7♥-4♠, the raiser bets and you raise. Everyone folds to the original raiser, who three-bets, you call. The turn is a 2♦. He bets, and you call. The river is the 4♦. He now checks. Do you bet?

Absolutely. Would he check A-A or K-K here? Maybe, but it's unlikely. He would check dozens of hand you can beat, like K-Q or J-J. He may have been putting you on a spade draw for his aggression on the flop, and is probably hoping for a free showdown, or a bluff from you with a missed draw. Most of the time your bet will elicit a call and will win. Winning limit poker is all about what happens most of the time.

River value bets are not limited to top pair, top kicker. After three limpers, you limp on the button with 9♣-9♦. The flop is J♠-7♠-6♦, an early player bets, a middle player calls and you call. This is not a raise or fold situation because of the intervening call. The turn is the 5♥, giving you a gutshot draw as well. The aggressor bets, middle player folds, and you elect to call. On the river, the 2♣, the player who has been betting suddenly checks. Should you bet?

Yes, you should. Maybe he has a jack, and you will lose. Yes, he might check a jack for reasons of his own, but more likely he does not have one. He either has busted draw, and it does not matter if you bet or not, or he has a hand like 8-7 and he is hoping for a free showdown. Don't give him one. Make him pay to see your hand. Again, over time, these bets show considerable profit and must be prominent in your arsenal.

Raising

Most players in position raise with big hands. Good. But there are other opportunities for raising, especially in tough games, which tend to elude average players. These include

1. Raising with A-K.
2. Raising probable value bets, including surprise lead bets.
3. Raising after slowplaying.

1. Raising with A-K

When you have an unimproved A-K, you may be tempted to call an opponent whom you suspect of bluffing. Unfortunately, sometimes he is bluffing with the best hand. Since you suspect him of bluffing in the first place or you would not be calling, raise! Yes, this costs you two bets when you are wrong, but it wins many pots against small pair bluffs and even value bets that get laid down. And if you are called, you gain a new measure of FUD. Now your big hands on the river may get paid off.

2. Raising probable value bets, including surprise lead bets

By far the best defence against the value bet is the raise in position. Make this play against tricky players who take advantage of scare cards to lead on the river, "knowing" you cannot raise for fear they hit their hand. Sure, sometimes they do, but often they are making an aggressive play out of position for fear that you have medium values and will check behind them. The point is, they are betting and planning to fold to a raise. Do not disappoint them. These raises are hugely profitable, and they tend to discourage these value bets on the river. As always, you must be aware of whom to make this play against, and what your image is. If you play a situational game, this raise in the right circumstance can gain whole pots.

3. Raising after slowplaying

Slowplaying to the river is another way to gain respect and make your opponents fear you. The criteria for making this play are covered in Chapter 24 – Raise the Turn or the River.

Folding

So far we have discussed offensive plays designed to make more money. They are important because the average player does not make enough of them.

Furthermore, limit poker does not favor the player who makes heroic laydowns on the river. Often the pot is large enough that you cannot be making a terrible error by calling.

All that said, you cannot simply call every time someone bets into you and you can beat a stone-cold bluff. Hand-reading and common sense come into play, as does an understanding of the price. Calling into a pot of eight big bets is not the same as calling into a pot of 25 big bets. In the first case, you need to be right more than12.5% of the time, in the latter, 4%. It is hard to judge the difference between 87.5% wrong and 96% wrong, but it makes a difference to your wallet.

Sometimes you can be virtually certain, even heads-up. Here are a couple of examples. You are on the button and limp after two others with A♠-3♠. The flop is Q♠-J♠-10♠. Everyone checks to you and you bet. The big blind and one limper call. After the 2♥ hits the turn, all check to you, you bet, and the big blind check-raises, the limper folds, you reraise and he calls. The river is the 5♦. BB checks, you bet and he check-raises again. This bothers you a bit, as you wonder what he can have since you have the ace-high flush and have pretty much told him that. But maybe he is confused or a non-believer and so you raise again. He four-bets. Should you call?

You probably will just out of frustration, but can you really have the best hand? You know he does not have the ace of spades, and he is still raising an unpaired board with three spades on it. If he is a decent, stable player, he has a straight flush. He has to. You know it. He cannot be bluffing, as he cannot expect you to lay down what he must know by now is the "nut flush". You can call, but you already know what you are going to see. Unless he is an amazing creative player (and you should be aware of this already), you are going to look at the straight flush you already know is there. It may not be 100%, but it sure is close. As tough as it is, you should fold here.

Let's look at a closer case. You have A♠-A♦ on the button and raise one middle position limper. The big blind and the limper call. You are not thrilled to see the flop of K♥-K♦- 7♣, but you bet after two checks. The big blind calls, and the limper raises. You figure this probably does not show a king, and you raise to get the big blind out, create dead money, and punish the limper who is trying to steal your pot. Also, their reactions to your raise will allow you to read their hands more easily.

Unexpectedly, the big blind calls again and the limper folds. What do you think the big blind has? There are no draws, and it is wildly unlikely that he is calling between two raisers with this board unless he has a king or better. Would anyone play Q-Q this way? Or A-7? No, he has a king (or 7-7) and is trying to be cute and hope you do not notice him. The turn is the 3♦ and he checks. You check behind him. The river is the 9♠. He bets. Do you call him?

You are getting 8-to-1 to call. Do you really believe you will win this pot more than 12.5% of the time? Do you believe you will have him beat ever? Maybe one time in a hundred or so he will be a player who has no clue what is going one and is playing his pocket fives or something (and you should know this about him as well). But if he is a normal player, he has you beat. You can place your pretty aces face down in the muck and save a big bet. This has been said many times before, but the bets you save spend just a well as the bets you win.

Once in a great while, you will make an incorrect laydown and the perpetrator will show you a bluff in an attempt to either show you how brilliant he is, or to get under your skin. Realizing you were outplayed may stir up all sorts of emotions in you, but do not let them affect your play in subsequent hands. The best players get bluffed once in a while. The worst players almost never get bluffed because they simply cannot lay down a hand. Simply add the fact that this player bluffed to your storehouse of knowledge about him, and go on trying to make the best decisions you can. And if that means you must fold another hand, so be it.

Multiway pots

Sometimes you will be in multiway hands even at the end. In general, these situations require more straightforward play then when you are heads-up. Bluff less, as the likelihood you will be called by at least one player goes up substantially. Value bet less for the same reason. Be more likely to believe players who lead from early position, as they realize that have to face multiple opponents, and any one of them may raise.

Hand reading is critical here. You need to piece together clues from the previous action. Luckily, in multiway pots, most players play more straightforwardly than in heads-up situations, and are therefore easier to read. Players who check in first position and call a bet rarely hold a good hand, as they would be reluctant to give up a free card. And if they held a very good hand, they could be check-raising. They most likely hold a draw of some kind. This becomes even more obvious when they check and cold-call a raise. Unless they have something close to the nuts, they are drawing. If the only likely draw gets there, and they lead out, they deserve respect.

There are a couple of plays worth mentioning that do not get much press:

- ♠ Raising to protect your hand from an overcall.
- ♠ The three-way bluff.

Raising to protect your hand from an overcall

Here is a rare play that you must nevertheless be aware of. You are in the middle in a three-way hand with a mediocre holding. A player who either has a very good hand or a bluff bets, most often from last position after the others had checked. You are now next to act. You realize that the bettor would check a decent holding to see if it is good, so he is either trying to buy the pot or has a big hand. If for any reason you suspect that he does not have a big hand, raise here.

The problem with calling is that the remaining player may have a mediocre holding that is better than yours, and he may also suspect a bluff. He reasons that you will call without a premium hand because you suspect the bettor is bluffing. If the pot is large, he is getting a good price to see whether his mediocre holding beats yours. Your raise will shut him out almost all the time. Yes, you will lose an extra bet when you are wrong, but you will save a whole pot once in a while. Your raise might even cause the bettor to fold a hand you could not beat, giving you an extra bonus.

The three-way bluff

I love this play, even though it comes up only once or twice a year. A player has been betting all the way and continues to bet on the river. The next player calls, generally somewhat reluctantly. You have nothing, having missed your draw. A raise here from a player with the right image (hopefully, you) will win a pot from good to excellent players who will "read" your hand and throw theirs away.

Here is an example: You hold 8♠-7♠ on the button. After four players limp in, you also call. The small blind completes, and the big blind raises. The flop is A♣-6♦-5♦, so you have an open-ended straight draw, although you worry about the diamonds. The big blind bets, two players call, and the next one raises. You call, getting 9.5-to-1. The big blind three-bets, two players fold, the raiser calls, as do you. The turn is the K♥.

Big blind bets, next player and you both call. The river is the 3♦. The big blind bets, the next player studies for a while and calls.

You must realize that to everyone but you, your plays so far have looked just like you were on a flush draw. You called all raises passively, which is just what a player with, say, Q♦-J♦ would have done. Against quality opponents, raising here has an excellent chance to win the pot. The big blind, who probably has a set or two pair, can easily "read" your hand for a flush and give it up, especially since he must worry that the caller may also have a flush. And the caller, who was reluctant to call the big blind, will be even more reluctant to throw good money after bad, especially now that he realizes that you must have him beat. This is a wonderful play, even though occasions for it happen seldom, and it does not work all the time. When it does work, you gain a huge pot and get to feel brilliant as well. And when is doesn't, well, you get some *Illusion of Action* points.

Conclusion

The river plays differently than the other streets, so be ready to make the adjustment. Decide before you see the river card how you will play if various cards hit. Avoid hesitations that come from, say, realizing you made your hand and don't know whether or not to bet.

Do not lose your aggression because the hand is almost over. Much of your profit will come from pots and bets you collect on the river from incorrect folds or crying calls. Keep up the pressure on your opponents, and become a feared competitor.

Chapter Twenty-Four

Raise the Turn or the River

In a hand played in the "Big Game" ($2,000-$4,000), Jennifer Harman held pocket aces in the small blind. Phil Hellmuth had raised from the cutoff, and Jennifer reraised. Phil elected to call. On the flop of K♠-4♦-4♥, Jennifer bet, Phil raised, and Jennifer called. She checked and called when the 8♠ came on the turn. On the river, the 5♦, Jennifer check-raised. Phil reraised, Jennifer called, and he showed pocket kings.

In his *CardPlayer* column, Phil wrote that Jennifer's check-raise on the river was an excellent play, as most players would raise the turn. Phil is correct both in his contention that Jennifer is a wonderful player and that she played the hand exceptionally well, even though she was unlucky and lost.

Upon reading this column, I decided to discuss the criteria that top players use to decide whether to raise on the turn or on the river when they believe they have the best hand. Because you would like to play like them, we will look at it from your perspective.

In general, look at these factors:

- ♠ The number of players.
- ♠ Your position.
- ♠ How aggressive your opponent is.

- ♠ The nature of the flop and turn.
- ♠ The hands you believe your opponent holds.
- ♠ What sort of scare cards can fall on the river.

The number of players

Always raise on the turn when you have the best hand and are facing two or more opponents. At least one of them will probably not be around to pay you off on the river, and you need to get the extra bets in now. Also, one of them could fold to your raise, making it more likely that you will win. Only when you are heads-up should you weigh the options of raising the turn or the river.

Your position

It is easier to delay your raise from the turn to the river in position. If your opponent bets the turn, you call, and he crosses you up and checks the river, you will get at least one bet in. If you are out of position and decide to check-raise the river, your opponent may check behind you so that you will collect nothing on that street. Jennifer's play out of position was much tougher than if she was in position, so she relied on some of the other factors.

How aggressive your opponent is

When you decide to wait to raise until the river, you are relying on your opponent to keep betting. The more aggressive he is, the more likely that this will happen. Some opponents fear the river so much that they tend to check almost no matter what hits. Against these players, you have to raise on the turn. On the other hand, others just keep bulling their way totally unfazed by scare cards or your calls or anything else. They believe they have the best hand and are willing to back it. If you raise the turn, some of them are good enough to realize they are beat and can make a good laydown, but they will call a raise on the river.

In addition, raising the river works well against frequent bluffers. In this case, a raise by you will shut them down. Waiting until the river gains you an extra bet against frequent bluffers while breaking even against aggressive players.

The nature of the flop and turn

If the flop presents few or no draws, your betting opponent is representing a made hand. If your hand is better than his, you can wait to raise on the river. In Phil's hand, the flop of K♠-4♦-4♥ seemed ideal for Jennifer's purpose. There was no chance Phil was on a draw. If the flop has many draws, and your opponent bets his draws, raise on the turn. He will always call because of the draw, and you want to get the extra bet while it is available. If your aggressive opponent bets his draws on the river after he misses them, you can wait for the river to raise. You were only going to collect two big bets anyway, and this way if he makes his draw and you read his hand well, you can save a bet by not raising on the river at all.

The hands you believe your opponent holds

If you wait for the river to raise, you must believe you have a good understanding of your opponent's tendencies and his likely holdings on this hand. The harder you find it to read his cards or intentions, the more often you should raise on the turn.

What sort of scare cards can fall on the river

This is perhaps the most important consideration, and I left it for last so we can examine it in more detail. Two kinds of scare cards can come:

- ♠ Those that scare the opponent into checking.
- ♠ Those that scare you into just calling.

On boards with many draws, raise the turn even if you are sure your opponent has a made hand instead of a draw. The problem is that if a draw gets there, it may scare your opponent into checking and cost you a bet even if that card did not improve either hand. If you were on a draw and made it on the turn, you should also probably raise. Again, the problem is that another card relevant to the draw may be irrelevant to you but may scare off your opponent.

For example, I have seen a number of players make the nut flush on the turn (say they hold A♦-5♦, the flop is K♦-6♣-3♦ and the turn is the 9♦) but flat call a turn bet, intending to raise the river. This works well when a blank hits, but if a fourth diamond comes, their opponent will check and possibly not even call. So they congratulate themselves on a clever play when no suited card comes, but miss bets when it does. In the long run, they are better off just raising on the turn.

Sometimes the river card can scare you because you were possibly drawn out on. In fact, this possibility is one of the key reasons to wait for the river to raise if all of the other signs align.

Looking at Jennifer's hand again, she probably put Phil on a big king for his pre-flop raise, call of the reraise, and raise on the flop. She was certain that Phil would bet his top pair excellent kicker throughout. The board had no draws, and no real scare card could come (except perhaps an unlikely ace) that would keep Phil from betting on the river. However, if a king hit on the river and Jennifer had not raised on the turn, she could simply check and call and see if her read was correct and Phil had outdrawn her. She would save a bet if Phil hit his two-outer, while still making her raise every time a blank hit.

Let's look at another situation. A player raises in middle position, and you three-bet with A-K. Everyone else folds. The flop comes A-6-3, he checks, you bet, and he check-raises. Almost certainly he has an ace here (or is representing one), and you hold the best kicker. You decide to call and wait for a later street to spring your trap. The turn is a deuce, almost certainly no help to either player. Your opponent bets, and you can raise here, but you should wait. He will certainly bet the river, and you can raise then. However, he probably has A-Q or A-J. Therefore, if a queen or jack hits on the river, you can simply call and see if he drew out. If anything else hits, you can raise for the same bet you would have won if you have raised on the turn.

Conclusion

Waiting until the river to raise is an advanced play because you need to be fairly certain that all of the factors are in your favor before you try it. If you are in doubt, just raise the turn.

However, if you learn to recognize the criteria and apply them properly, selective raising on the river can be an effective way to save a few bets and win a few extra ones. And you may find it fun to surprise your opponent on the river once in a while. Just don't run into Phil and his flopped full house too often.

Epilogue

Forgive Yourself

Whenever you play poker, you will make errors. As you expand your game beyond the standard hands and start to play positional, people-oriented, situational poker, you will make more. These extra errors will happen because you will be in more ambiguous and difficult situations, and you will therefore get more wrong.

Of course, you will also get some right, and your overall results will improve. However, the wrong ones can cause you to doubt or even to blame yourself. You will think, "If only I had not played that hand (or made that raise or run that bluff or called that bet), I would not have lost that money."

It is okay to think that, of course, as long as you don't let it affect your mental state. But it is easy to get down on yourself, to stop playing aggressively, or to revert to more straightforward methods. A positive attitude is essential to make the plays and keep up the pressure on your opponents that will ultimately result in your greater success, especially when the opposition gets tougher.

The most important thing to remember is the need to forgive yourself. The next hand you play is the only one that matters, and hands in the past are not important except as they affect your image and your understanding of how your opponents perceive you. Your task is to make the best decision now, integrating all the information you have about your opponents and their perception of you. Errors are inevitable in a game of incomplete information; your response to them is within your control. The better you get at not dwelling on past mistakes other than to learn from them and move on, the better your play will be.

To summarize, *play your best, pay attention, make plays when the situation dictates, and forgive yourself when you get it wrong*. Put all of this together and you will have fun *and* make money, which is what makes poker so wonderful.

Poker books from D&B

Poker 24/7
by Stewart Reuben
978-1-904468-16-5, 256pp, $24.95 / £15.99

Poker on the Internet
by Andrew Kinsman
978-1-904468-20-2, 208pp, $19.95 / £12.99

Beginners Guide to Limit Hold'em
by Byron Jacobs
978-1-904468-21-9, 208pp, $19.95 / £12.99

How Good is Your Limit Hold 'em?
by Byron Jacobs with Jim Brier
978-1-904468-15-8, 192pp, $23.95 / £13.99

How Good is Your Pot-Limit Omaha?
by Stewart Reuben
978-1-904468-07-3, 192pp, $19.95 / £12.99

How Good is Your Pot-Limit Hold'em?
by Stewart Reuben
978-1-904468-08-0, 208pp, $19.95 / £12.99

Hold'em on the Come
by Rolf Slotboom and Drew Mason
978-1-904468-23-3, 272pp, $19.95 / £12.99

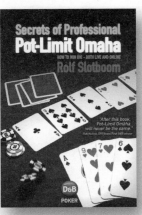

Secrets of Professional Pot-Limit Omaha
by Rolf Slotboom
978-1-904468-30-6, 240pp, $24.95 / £14.99

Limit Hold'em: Winning short-handed strategies
by Terry Borer and Lawrence Mak with Barry Tannenbaum
978-1-904468-37-0, 352pp, $24.95 / £14.99